language teaching

Editorial

The journal aims to help people concerned with the teaching and learning of languages to keep up to date with the latest findings in research, language studies and applied linguistics. Work carried out in different parts of the world and reported in different languages is made accessible by means of abstracts written in English.

Members of the Editorial Board scan some 400 journals from many countries in order to select and abstract the most useful and significant articles. Most of the abstracts are specially written by a team of abstractors who are specialists in the subjects concerned. Where author or journal abstracts are used, they may be edited in keeping with this journal's policy to present the author's arguments and findings. It is therefore not essential for readers to have access to the original articles, though these may be consulted at the CILT or British Council libraries (see facing page for details). Photocopies of articles may be obtained by libraries or individuals in the usual manner through the International Photocopy Service of the British Library Lending Division, Boston Spa, Wetherby, West Yorkshire, United Kingdom, LS23 7BQ.

How to use the journal

The abstracts are divided into four main subject areas; Language learning and teaching – theory and practice; Teaching particular languages; Research in the supporting sciences, and Language description and use. These subject areas are subdivided into several different categories, and abstracts arranged alphabetically by author's name within each category.

A full list of the periodicals scanned appears in each January issue. Asterisks denote periodicals from which articles were abstracted in the preceding year. Initials show whether the periodical is kept in the CILT or British Council library.

The heading for each abstract gives the author's name, and his affiliation if this was given in the original article. The title of the article is given in the language of the original article, with an English translation in square brackets if necessary. All abstracts are written in English.

Subject and author indexes appear in each issue, and are cumulated annually in the October issue.

State of the art (survey) articles

Recent titles: Language testing; Communicative theory and its influence on materials production; English for Academic Purposes (EAP); Pedagogical grammar; Computer-assisted language learning; Contrasting discourses – contrastive analysis and a discourse approach to writing.

Forthcoming topics: Self-access; language and gender.

In the next issue: New technologies in ELT by Jack Lonergan.

Copying

This journal is registered with the Copyright Clearance Center, 27 Congress Street, Salem, Mass. 01970. Organisations in the USA who are also registered with C.C.C. may therefore copy material (beyond the limits permitted by sections 107 and 108 of US copyright law) subject to payment to C.C.C. of the per-copy fee of $5.00. This consent does not extend to multiple copying for promotional or commercial purposes. Code 0261-4448/90 $5.00 + .00.

ISI Tear Sheet Service, 3501 Market Street, Philadelphia, Pennsylvania 19104, USA, is authorised to supply single copies of separate articles for private use only.

For all other use, permission should be sought from the Cambridge or New York offices of the Cambridge University Press.

Subscriptions

Four issues of language teaching (ISSN 0261-4448) (published in January, April, July and October) form a volume. A complete volume may be purchased at the subscription price (which includes postage) if payment is made before publication of the volume is complete. The subscription price of Volume 23, 1990, is £38.00 net (USA $79.00 in USA and Canada) for institutions, £41.00 elsewhere; £19.00 (USA $39.00 in USA and Canada) for individuals when ordering direct from the Press and certifying that the journal is for their personal use. Single parts cost £11 (USA $24.00 in USA and Canada) plus postage. Orders, which must be accompanied by payment, may be sent to a bookseller or to Cambridge University Press, The Edinburgh Building, Shaftesbury Road, Cambridge CB2 2RU or in the USA or Canada, to Cambridge University Press, The Journals Department, 40 West 20th Street, New York, NY 10011, USA. Second class postage paid at New York, NY and at additional mailing offices. POSTMASTER: send address changes in USA and Canada to language teaching, Cambridge University Press, 110 Midland Avenue, Port Chester, New York, NY 10573.

State of the art article

Learner language

Carl James *University of Wales, Bangor*

My title is as neutral as possible: it is intended to cover roughly the same areas as those covered by Corder's (1975; reprinted 1978) state-of-the-art survey under the title 'Error analysis, interlanguage and second language acquisition'. The useful distinction that used to be drawn (Christophersen, 1973) between 'second' and 'foreign' languages seems now to have been abandoned in favour of 'second', as evidenced by the title of one of the most successful British textbooks for the field, *Understanding second language acquisition* (Ellis, 1985), and the name of the recently formed *European Second Language Association* (EUROSLA). This is unfortunate, since most European work concerns *foreign* language teaching and learning. Equally important, the claim is legitimately made that much of the American *second* language research which is based on data from Spanish speaking immigrants or overseas students in American colleges (Dulay, Burt & Krashen, 1982; Robinett & Schachter, 1983) makes claims which are probably untrue for, and not generalisable to, *foreign* language teaching situations: for example, the claim made by Dulay *et al.* (*op. cit.*) that only three per cent of errors are attributable to first-language interference. Another related distinction I shall overlook initially but return to eventually is that between *acquisition*, which takes place in 'naturalistic' environments like streets, playgrounds and the workplace, and *learning* which is done in classrooms. A third distinction worth making is that between *acquisition* and *development* drawn by Chomsky (1980) in the course of a discussion of first language knowledge but illuminatingly extrapolated to 'second' language by Cook (1988). Language *development* takes place over time and as such is the basis of the longitudinal studies that have provided the bulk of the data in this field; *acquisition* on the other hand is what Chomsky calls a 'logical problem' since it concerns explaining how a complex phenomenon like human language is learnable in principle, not describing how it is learnt in real time.

According to Corder (1973), description of a language, be it that of a native speaker or of a raw learner, is a first-order application of linguistics. Description is necessary before we can move on to the second-order application of linguistics: comparison. In learner language applied linguistics there are three codes to describe: the learner's native language (NL), the target language (TL, a term neutral between 'second' and 'foreign') and the learner's version of the TL, her interlanguage (IL, from Selinker, 1972) or 'idiosyncratic dialect' (Corder, 1971). Moving on to the second-order applications, we can compare these three pairwise. Comparing NL and TL is known as contrastive analysis or CA (James, 1980); comparing IL with TL is error analysis or EA (Norrish, 1983); and lastly, comparing NL with IL with the intention of identifying any traces of NL in IL is called transfer analysis or TA (Kellerman, 1987; Odlin, 1989). While not denying outright what Bley-Vroman (1983) calls the 'comparative fallacy' in interlanguage studies, that is 'the mistake of studying the systematic character of one language [IL] by comparing it to another [TL]', the present survey will take a closer look at each of these last three types of comparative study, which I refer to collectively in the title as 'learner language'.

1. Contrastive analysis

The 'classical' Contrastive Analysis Hypothesis claims that the potential negative transfers from NL on to the TL can be predicted by juxtaposing descriptions of comparable systems and subsystems of the two languages. Information about the contrasts thus identified can be incorporated into pedagogic materials and imparted to FL teachers so that this potential NL interference can be deactivated and the incidence of errors arising from this source minimised (Fisiak, ed., 1981). By the mid-1970s the CA hypothesis was under attack, most menacingly from those who, working mainly in a second-language (immigrant) setting, saw little unequivocal proof of NL interference, for example among Chinese and Spanish children acquiring English in the USA (Dulay *et al.*, 1982). More generally, the predictive power of CAs was shown to be limited, some items of high interlingual contrastivity proving to be easily learnt, and some items of low or no contrastivity proving difficult. It was consequently felt that the promise could not be kept of delivering a scale of learning difficulty based on the analysis of language differences and CA was reluctantly abandoned by many of its erstwhile followers.

There was a modest but significant revival of confidence in CA in the early 1980s, attributable to a variety of causes. In his monograph *Contrastive analysis*, James (1980) challenged the validity of some of the criticism that had been levelled against CA and appears to have dispelled some misunderstandings, e.g. the false assumption that NL interference was either the sole or at least the main cause of learning difficulty. Then CA assumed a more positively optimistic tone when the potentials for positive or facilitative NL transfer were given more attention by scholars like Ringbom (1987),

State of the art: Learner language

who compared the positive as well as the negative transfers made by Swedish Finns learning English (a language cognate with their Swedish NL) and Finnish (a distant one). He discovered that the facilitation derived from learning a related language comes in the form of increased comprehension in the early stages: since, as Krashen (1982) has insisted, 'comprehensible input' is so vital to acquisition, early comprehension confers a great boon. There followed the observation that learners are not automata who just transfer NL forms mechanically and unthinkingly: Kellerman (1978) suggested that learners have intuitions about what is transferable from their NL to any specific TL, that is, learners are guided by their 'psychotypology', which constitutes their belief about the cognateness of the two languages (NL and TL) and the language-specificity of the linguistic unit in question. His suggestion is that marked elements of NL are not transferable. He defines marked elements as those which are '...infrequent, irregular, semantically or structurally opaque, or in any other way exceptional'.

While Kellerman invoked psychotypology to explain failures of plain CAs to predict with accuracy, others referred to syntactic markedness. Echman (1977) pointed out that NL and TL may possess a feature in common, so that there is apparently no contrast and consequently no potential interference, but as that feature is more marked (cf. Kellerman's definition above) there is contrast after all. Zobl (1986) suggested that English has unmarked word order (Subject+Verb+Object), which the speaker of English is happy to transfer to French, resulting in erroneous forms such as *Le chien a mangé les*. By contrast, the French native speaker will never try to transfer his marked Subject+Pronoun Object+Verb construction to English. This observation explains why such learners do not produce errors like *He them likes*.

Paradoxically, it has been the influence of Chomsky's (1981) theory of 'Universal Grammar' and the associated idea that language particulars are the reflection of selections from a fixed set of parameters that has helped to revitalise CA: 'paradoxical' in that it took a theory of universals of language to shed light on language idiosyncrasies (Rutherford, 1984). Flynn (1984) studied Japanese learners resetting their NL head-initial parameter on learning TL English, where heads are non-initial in the phrase. She compared their learning with that of Spanish NL speakers, who did not have to reset this parameter on learning English. So what we used to refer to as structural transfer is now seen as changing the plus and minus values of parameters, rather like altering the DIP switches on a computer printer. The most studied parameter however has been the *Pro-Drop Parameter* (White, 1985) which determines whether a language can or cannot delete its subject pronouns as does Portuguese: *Conheço bem este senhor* [know+1st Singular Inflexion+well this gentleman]. Such an isolated observation is of no great significance, but parameterised grammars do not stop at the isolated observation. Their great strength is that they associate phenomena which hitherto have been viewed as discrete. Thus, if a language does delete its subject pronouns it will also, among other features: allow inversion of its subject noun phrases (*Chegou o meu pai*) [Arrived the my father]; have inflected modals (*Não posso comer ostras*) [no can+1st Singular Infl+eat oysters]; and lack expletives like English 'It...' or 'There...' sentence initially (*Parece que ela não gosta da comida*) [ø seems that she no likes the food]. This suggests that a long-cherished goal of CA is now at last within reach: bundles of associated concomitant contrasts can be identified and sets of predictions made all at once, since each such phenomenon implicates others. Hawkins (1986) has shown how it is possible to use such implicational relationships to associate contrasts between German and English syntax that have been known about for some time but have hitherto been seen as unrelated. CA can only be as powerful as the linguistic theory upon which it is predicated (James, 1980): we now see that with the development of Chomskyan syntax there is a scope for parallel development in CA. However, in view of the enormous technical sophistication of modern syntax, CA is no longer easy to do and is not for the faint-hearted.

CA has also been revitalised by widening its perspective beyond the sentence, so there are now flourishing new domains: contrastive rhetoric, pragmatics, discourse and text analysis (Hartmann, 1980). Contrastive rhetoric, where the focus is on contrasts in culturally-determined writing conventions, has enjoyed most attention, starting with Kaplan's (1966) speculations on the general tendencies of argument-structure in Semitic, Oriental, Romance, Slav and Anglo-Saxon texts. Though at its inception speculative and ethnocentric (through its apparent suggestion that Anglo-Saxon rhetoric is the most direct, scientific and suited to the modern world), this theory was the starting point for a great deal of serious CA study on Japanese v. English (Hinds, 1983; Jenkins & Hinds, 1987; Oi, 1986; Shimozaki, 1985) and Arabic v. English (Johnstone-Koch, 1983; Al-Jubouri, 1984; Ostler, 1987). There is a useful survey by Houghton and Hoey (1983) and the anthologies edited by Connor and Kaplan (1987) and Purves (1988). Contrastive pragmatics involves the identification of cross-cultural differences in speech act realisations, conversational routines such as service encounters (Ventola, 1983) in the pursuit of insights concerning how the native language influences TL communicative competence (Richards & Sukiwiwat, 1985). Its beginnings were in the work done on German–English (House &

Kasper, 1981). A theoretical framework for the study of NL-induced pragmalinguistic failure was proposed by Thomas (1983). It has focused on ways of being polite in different language communities: House and Kasper (1981) show that Germans tend to make their requests more direct than the English do, while Blum-Kulka (1982) makes the same observation for Israelis as compared to Americans. Other speech acts that have been studied contrastively are: Apologies (Coulmas, 1981), Compliments (Wolfson, 1989; Herbert, 1989), telephone-call openings in France and the USA (Godard, 1977), and others reported in House and Blum-Kulka (1986), Oleksy (1989) and Odlin (1989).

2. Transfer analysis

The reinstatement of CA has, however, only been apparent and a high price has been exacted. Long ago Wardhaugh (1970) pointed out that the CA hypothesis can exist in two versions: a 'strong' version that claims to be able to predict learning difficulty on the basis of a previously executed contrastive (NL:TL) description, and a 'weak' version that makes the more modest claim of only being able to explain a subset of attested errors as resulting from transfer from the NL. CA is no longer much practised in 'applied' linguistics circles in its strong version. It has had to give way to the description and explanation of actually occurring NL transfers. This has led to an uncertain relabelling, and we seem to be left with the option of referring to 'crosslinguistic influence' (Kellerman & Sharwood Smith, 1986) or to 'language transfer' (Gass & Selinker, 1983). Recent work in NL transfer in FL learning has in fact moved the centre of gravity over toward error analysis. TA is in fact a subdiscipline within EA which rests upon the assumption that certain deviances in learner production are the result of NL transfers. That this assumption is often unwarranted is all too often forgotten, since the only way to test any assumption of NL transfer is to do an old-style predictive CA before undertaking the TA. TAs are in fact edifices built upon straw foundations, deceptive shortcuts that merely lead you back to where you set out from. They are also part of EA, since they deal with attested rather than predicted deviance. It is to EA that we now turn our attention.

3. Error analysis

There is a constant tension between the descriptive and long-term explanatory priorities of those engaged in IL studies and contrastive analysis research on the one hand and the shorter-term pedagogic priorities of EA on the other. Expediency is the scourge of the applied linguist. There has also been a much greater volume of publication in IL studies than in EA: in the latter, only three short book-length works have appeared in recent years: Norrish (1983) is a short and clear introduction for teachers to the practical aspects of EA; Swan and Smith (1986) is a listing of the main problems encountered by 18 NL groups when they learn English, not so much an analysis as a legacy of teachers' experience with those groups of learners; and Edge (1989), an altogether more substantial work in content if not in bulk, to which we shall return presently. There has been a virtual cessation of work on relative error gravities. Johansson (1978) identified those foreignisms in the English of Swedes that tend to be irritants: apparently native speakers of English tolerate the misdistribution of the clear and dark allophones of /l/ but do not take kindly to foreigners who substitute their own velar fricative [R] for the English frictionless continuant [ɹ]. Albrechtsen, Henriksen and Faerch (1980) made complementary findings: just as foreignisms can irritate natives, so can nativisms. Perhaps being too native is seen as presumptuous on the part of the learner. They found that English natives were irritated by advanced foreign learners' excessive recourse to very English conversational gambits and fillers such as: *sort of, kinda, know what I mean? you bet, pull the other one*. Likewise the use of paraphrase is not always well received: the learner who produced 'things that come on TV every week' to compensate for ignorance of the word 'serial' was also seen as irritating. The greatest irritants to native speakers then are not grammar or morphology errors (the first obsession of classical EA) but what Thomas (1983) calls 'pragmatic failures', most of which seem to result from NL transfers: so, in Russia, according to Thomas, you can stop someone in the street and directly command *Give me a cigarette, comrade* or in a bus directly order someone to pass you a ticket. English would employ less direct language, using such 'softeners' as *would you..., I wonder..., would you mind...*

Davies (1983) develops some ideas discussed by James (1977) and by Hughes and Lascaratu (1982) on differences in gravity ratings of errors made by different groups of judges: teachers, non-teachers, native speakers and non-native speakers of the TL. The native speakers tended in all cases to greater leniency. She suggests that the foreign teacher's deprecatory assessment of learner error is likely to reflect her teaching experience, her own proficiency in the TL, plus a feeling that she herself is being tested for her ability to spot errors and express suitable disparagement of them.

A general reluctance has developed to adopt a judgemental, normative stance toward learner errors. This attitude was already present at the inception of IL studies, when it was suggested that a learner's IL is a natural human language (Adjemian, 1977) and ought to be accorded the dignity it

State of the art: Learner language

merits, not compared to the ideal native speaker's version and found to be wanting. This continues to be an unresolved issue in EA. It arises whenever we ask what the learner's erroneous version is to be compared with: with what a native speaker would say, or with what the learner ought to be able to say? The refusal to take native-speaker forms as the standard against which to describe IL leads to a refusal to take these norms for evaluating IL. A number of developments in linguistics have contributed to this widespread reluctance to condemn error. Let us look at some of these:

(i) Variability

IL is a natural human language and as such is likely to be variable: just as native speakers of English vacillate between *It has to be Harry* and *It must be Harry*, or the two alternative pronunciations of *secretary*, so learners sometimes produce TL-like forms, sometimes not. We do not censure natives for the variability of their language, so why do we censure learners? The suggestion that IL operates on variable rather than fixed or 'categorial' rules (L. J. Dickerson, 1975; W. B. Dickerson, 1977) is well summarised by Littlewood (1981) and by Tarone (1983, 1988). Littlewood identifes three different types of learner according to the learner's access to instruction and adherence to TL norms. These ideas are further developed in Selinker and Douglas (1985), suggesting that learners create 'discourse domains' or 'contexts within which...IL structures are created differentially'. Tarone and Parrish (1988) develop this idea, showing how different types of task determine different accuracy levels for just one category: the article. As a result we ought not to expect an individual's IL to develop uniformly across all such domains but differentially in each. Context is but one determinant of variation. Another is the availability of norms; their availability can be externally arranged (by the fact that one is working in a classroom, with teacher and such reference sources at hand), or one happens to know the relevant rule explicitly or metalinguistically, so that one is in a position to monitor one's own production. The monitor model (Krashen, 1981, 1982) has exerted considerable influence on thinking about IL. The co-existence of erroneous and correct forms of the same target in IL is now viewed as normal, whereas before such inconsistency was taken as proof of the learner's carelessness. The 'gradual diffusion' model of variability (Gatbonton, 1983) suggests that learning proceeds in two phases: first, correct forms co-exist with incorrect; then the incorrect are expunged, to be replaced by the correct. But the second stage is dependent on the previous one: errors are therefore a necessary step in the learning process.

(ii) Infelicities

The idea that one can use language 'infelicitously' without being wrong stems from Austin's seminal work on the execution and misexecution of performative speech acts. As CA, as we have seen above, gradually gave way to transfer analysis, so it became normal to think of learners not so much committing error as misexecuting (*vis-à-vis* native-speaker performance) a speech act, and so appearing to be brusque, ungrateful, or in some other way impolite or awkward. Such judgements reflect the essential difference between the rules of phonology and morphosyntax of a language on the one hand and the tendencies and conventions of its discourse on the other: the former is relatively fixed, so error there is easily identified, while the latter appears to be less catagorical, more a matter of tendencies and of infelicities. But the idea that learners produce forms which, even if corrected, are not quite what the native would say is developed by Levenston (1978). He shows that an EA that limits itself to reconstruction, i.e. on putting the grammar right, is flawed: what is left will still display lexical inadequacy, syntactic blends, conceptual confusion and rhetorical ineptitude. We could say that what learners write may well be discourse 'in English' but still falls short of being 'English discourse'. The attention has shifted, then, from clear-cut error to the vaguer notion of infelicity. Once again the issue arises of what to compare the learner's production with: the native speaker's version or what the learner was aiming for.

(iii) Advanced learners

Much of the early work on IL, which indicated that there were universal orders of acquisition that had little to do with the native language of the learner or with the sort of teaching he received, was based on young learners in the early stages of learning English. This was to some extent a reflection of the tendency for SLA researchers to follow in the footsteps of child language researchers like Brown (1973) and de Villiers and de Villiers (1978). There has been a shift in focus recently, with the spotlight now on the advanced learner (Coleman & Towell, 1986; Dechert & Lennon, 1989; Lennon, 1989 and in press). The reasons for the shift are elusive and complex, but one is connected with the implication which can be drawn from work such as Levenston's (*op. cit.*): that many of the problems faced by learners are not limited to FL learners at all, but are problems that beset native speakers as well. Hymes' 'communicative competence' is not something that natives possess but learners lack: in some natives, too, it is conspicuously lacking. Nor do all native speakers write well, and Shaughnessy (1977) has observed that for some individuals who have consummate control of the spoken mode, learning to write literally involves learning a new language. Dechert and Lennon (*op. cit.*) contend that natives and learners alike produce blend errors such as **a new time low* (a coalescence of *all-time low* and *new low*) as a consequence of cognitive overload. If the line between native speakers and non-natives has to be drawn, the first logical move is to see how natives and near-native advanced learners differ. This has not proved easy, which means that we should be more cautious than traditional EA has been before talking about the errors in anybody's IL.

(iv) International English

The title of an early classic in EA was *Common errors in Gold Coast English* (Brown & Scragg, 1948). Sey (1974) described Ghanaian English in its own right, not in terms of error, and nowadays nobody would seriously think of designating the differences between, say, British English and any of the 'colonial' varieties of English as 'errors'. There has been in recent years an extension of this tendency to view all varieties of a language, metropolitan, colonial and non-native, as being of equal validity, a line of thought on the international arena which has paralleled the national debate over standard English in Britain that raged with the publication of Honey's (1983) political and provocative monograph on the deterioration of standards of English in Britain's schools; this was discussed in the context of a centrally imposed National Curriculum in the *Kingman Report* (1988).

There is no denying that English is an international language, and as such we must expect to encounter a multitude of local varieties: not only the national Englishes, such as American, British, Australian, etc. but also an even greater number of learner Englishes, such as French English, Brazilian English, Japanese English and the like. But the analogy between these two types of varieties must not be forced; while it would be absurd to condemn American English 'faucet' or 'Do you have children?' as errors, the same should not be said for Spanish 'a real (royal) prince' or German English 'We smoke not here'. In this vein, Quirk (1989) finds it odd that Bartsch admits to having written her book *Norms of language* (1987) '...in the German variety of English...one of the many varieties of the supervariety International English'. Notice the sleight of hand: the reasonable observation that English is an international language has been upgraded to the dubious assumption that there is a *language* called 'International English', a claim that begs many a question, such as: What are the norms of this language? Who are its native speakers? What are its origins? How are its varieties (or dialects) circumscribed? Davies (1989) asks whether English as an International Language (EIL) is an IL: they are both simplified, he contends, the former in terms of function, the latter in terms of form. A serious study of the sociolinguistic status of the foreigner's language is Janicki (1985). It is said that the ultimate arbiter of the question of what language or dialect an individual is speaking is that individual's own belief: the fact that so many speakers of this International English consider themselves to be speakers of one of its nonstandard dialects is sufficient reason for us to concede that some of the forms they use are errors. Such learners have trouble enough understanding the native-speaker dialects and accents of British English (Hughes & Trudgill, 1986); if the many regional learner dialects are to be nurtured in the way that some suggest, global intelligibility will deteriorate and English will cease to be serviceable as an international language.

(v) Learner strategies

One consequence of the replacement of behaviourist learning theory in applied linguistics by the cognitive theory was to view the language learner as an intelligent, discriminating decision-maker, matching means and ends in learning and in communicating; he became a strategy user (Faerch & Kasper, 1983; Wenden & Rubin, 1987). Although 'strategy' has never been adequately defined in the learner language literature, and although some bizarre labels are given to learner behaviour, such as 'the strategy of incorrect application' (Tarone, Frauenfelder & Selinker, 1976), it has been widely exemplified, and it comes over as an altogether positive concept: learners deploying strategies or teachers encouraging learners to use their existing strategies and add more to their strategy repertoires, seem assured of receiving an accolade. Innumerable dissertations describing learner strategies are written annually in universities world-wide. This stance has two consequences: the first is that learners get credit for having not learnt, when they use the avoidance, coinage or paraphrase strategies to conceal their ignorance of TL forms they might otherwise have learnt; the second is that errors are explained away as mere superficial manifestations of underlying good language learner behaviour. This double-think is not limited to linguistics: apparently economists distinguish 'underlying' inflation (which is low) from visible inflation (which is uncomfortably high).

On the positive side, the study of learner strategies has drawn two very useful distinctions. The first distinction is that between *learning* (or 'code breaking') strategies on the one hand and *communication* (or encoding) strategies on the other (Faerch & Kasper, *op. cit.*). The second distinction is between two sorts of communication strategies: there are encoding or production strategies and there are decoding or receptive strategies. In early work on EA, there was an assumption that errors were exclusively of the first type: certainly none of the error taxonomies proposed, by Selinker (1972), Richards (1974), Wode (1979) or Dulay *et al.* (1982), referred to errors in reception, errors that result in misinterpretation. This imbalance has been righted in work by Hosenfeld (1977), Urquart (1984), and Laufer and Sim (1985).

(vi) Error correction

We referred in the introduction to the learning-acquisition dichotomy. This is Krashen's (1983) version of the distinction originally drawn by Palmer (1921) between 'conscious assimilation [when] we learn without knowing that we are learning' (*op. cit.*, 44) as opposed to the sort of learning for which we take recourse to our 'studial capacities' (*ibid.*, 127). Of the two ways to internalise a language, acquisition has been assumed to be the superior, the reasons being perhaps first, that it is natural and 'doing what comes naturally' is inherently good; and second, that children acquire the NL with a 100% success rate without the help of teachers. Learning is demoted to second best, a resource for 'substitute utterance initiation', a source of consciously learnt rules for monitoring one's performance, a cosmetic to cover up lack of true acquisition: 'a cure, but not a very permanent one' (Krashen, 1983: 146), since 'using the conscious Monitor will only cover up the error temporarily' (Krashen, 1985: 48). The claim that conscious knowledge of rules, and conscious awareness that one has just broken one (and committed an error), does nothing to advance one's true command of the FL is known as the 'No Interface' position. It has been attacked from all sides (James, in press) and shows signs of giving way to a Weak Interface position (Sharwood Smith, 1981) which would endorse reference to grammatical explanation and other means of consciousness raising (James & Garrett, in press), while not denying the value of acquisition-rich environments for FL development, where these can be created or exploited. No-one nowadays would want to defend a hard-line Strong Interface position, which would claim that acquisition comes only from conscious Learning.

This issue of the role of consciousness in acquisition is of course crucial when we come to consider the applications of the findings of EA in teaching. Upon discovering errors among his learners the teacher can covertly revise or reteach the problematic point and is free to use inductive techniques to promote acquisition this time round. But that may fail for a second or third time and the teacher will have to consider the deductive, explicit teaching of the point: whether to give learners feedback on their errors and, if so, how to phrase a grammatical explanation (Long, 1977). It is argued by Chaudron (1988) that teacher feedback to the learner allows the latter to confirm or reject her hypotheses about the rules of the TL. This feedback can take two forms, known as negative or positive feedback or, as Chomsky (1981: 8–9) terms them in his account of caregiver feedback to infants acquiring the NL: positive v. negative 'evidence'. Infants get 'positive' evidence from hearing actual instances in the speech around them of patterns they might be in doubt over; they could in principle also get 'negative' evidence which is direct and comes in the form of correction of their errors by adults. But Chomsky rejects the idea that provision of direct negative evidence is necessary for NL acquisition. This does not mean, though, that it is unnecessary or not helpful in FL learning. Indeed, error correction such as happens in FL classrooms is the teacher's main resource. Of course, as Chaudron (1988) stresses, in order to avoid a defensive reaction on the learner's part, whereupon he would raise his 'affective filter' (Krashen, 1983), the correcting move must be executed sensitively. In his review of literature on the issue of error correction, Chaudron (*op. cit.*) makes the following points: learners want to be corrected; errors on an area of the TL in current pedagogic focus should get priority; teachers tend to let pass the most frequent errors – just the ones that should not be ignored; teacher correction and explanation of error can lead to dramatic improvement, in the short term as well as the long term. This last point should encourage the teacher.

Mention was made above of the decisions teachers have to make about what, when and how to correct and make remedial intervention. In this context, the distinction drawn by Corder (1967) between error and mistake in IL has regularly resurfaced as a conceptual issue in EA. Bialystok and Sharwood Smith (1985) draw essentially the same distinction when they speak of 'knowledge' on the one hand and 'control' on the other: inadequacy in knowledge results in error, lack of control in mistake. Taylor (1986) in a discussion owing much to Shaugnessy (1977) about giving feedback to writers, raises the problem of determining 'whether a mistake is a slip or a genuine error'. He argues that native speakers will not make an error over the 3rd person singular ending -*s*, but might well omit it as a slip. Johnson (1988) takes this idea a step further when he argues that FL learning involves 'procedural' knowledge and skills training and so is about avoiding or correcting mistakes: it is not about errors, to which we have paid too much attention. He goes on to propose four conditions for mistakes correction. Edge (1989) likewise attempts a refinement of the nomenclature: for him, 'mistake' is the generic term, subtypes of which are 'errors', 'slips' and 'attempts'. Each of these has a different status and ought to receive different treatment from teachers. He takes an extremely tolerant attitude to 'mistakes' (deviance in IL), perhaps captured in his claim that 'correction should mean helping people to become more accurate, not insisting on completely standard English' (*op. cit.*, 50). Errors being mainly atomic, which means locatable to a fine distinction, surely to be 'better' is generally synonymous with being completely standard. Edge also defends the idea that error making is necessary if learners are to learn 'better rules': I would suggest, though, that they can work out better rules if they do not commit themselves (or their error) but instead keep quiet or imitate lots of 'positive' evidence.

(vii) Broader perspectives

We are encouraged to do interdisciplinary research. There appears to be scope for this in EA, but it has not materialised, probably on account of academic insularity. This is unfortunate, since there are connections there waiting to be made. For example, there is work that is germane to EA going on in Writing research (Shaughnessy, 1977; Perera, 1984; Purves, 1988). Then in the field of Instructional Science we find useful discussions of 'error factors' and how these are manifest during mathematics lerning, for instance, when learners hypothesise 'mal-rules' and succumb to 'bugs': Lewis (1981); Pickthorne (1983); Priest (1981). In mother tongue education for Basic Literacy we note the emergence of 'miscue analysis', which is concerned with the reader's reliance on contextual information (Potter, 1980). The analysis and evaluation of Linguistic prescriptivism are perennial concerns in linguistics: we have mentioned Honey (1983) and the furore it raised. Sunby and Bjørge (1983) report on a project aiming to collect and codify the forms of English which were stigmatised by early English grammarians, thus adding a historical perspective to error judgements. In the field of Translation evaluation, concerns familiar to the student of EA have been to the fore in work such as House and Blum-Kulka (1986) and Lörscher (1987).

In this survey I hope to have revealed four simple truths about the field. First, that there is a colossal and very complex field of study that aims to describe, explain, and ultimately predict the specific and universal features of learner language. Second, that attempts to compartmentalise this field and enhance the status of some activities within it are short-sighted if they serve anything other than expository convenience. Third, that old wine does come in new bottles (or vice-versa) and some of the purported innovations in the field (error/mistake, learning/acquisition, contrast/transfer) ought to be venerated with the respect due to age, but not heralded as breathtaking new breakthroughs. Finally, I hope to have suggested at least that there are no easy solutions for direct application to the classroom, but rather, as Bernard Spolksy (1970) urged some years ago, potential insights and implications that lie latent for those who have the patience to look beneath the surface of learner language.

References

ALBRECHTSEN, D., HENRIKSEN, B. & FAERCH, C. (1980). Native speaker reactions to learners' spoken interlanguage. *Language Learning*, 30 (2), 365–96.
AUSTIN, J. L. (1962). *How to do things with words*. Oxford: Oxford University Press.
ADJEMIAN, C. (1976). On the nature of interlanguage systems. *Language Learning*, 26, 297–320.
ALDERSON, J. C. & URQUART, A. H. (eds.) (1984). *Reading in a foreign language*. London: Longman.
AL-JUBOURI, A. J. R. (1984). The role of repetition in Arabic argumentative discourse. In J. Swales & M. Hassan (eds.).
BAILYSTOK, E. & SHARWOOD SMITH, M. (1985). Interlanguage is not a state of mind *Applied Linguistics*, 5, 2.
BLEY-VROMAN, R. (1983). The comparative fallacy in interlanguage studies. *Language Learning*, 33, 1–17.
BLUM-KULKA, S. (1982). Learning to say what you mean in a second language: a study of the speech act performances of learners of Hebrew as a second language. *Applied Linguistics*, 3, 1, 29–59.
BROWN, H. D. (ed.) (1976). Papers in second language acquisition. *Language Learning* (special issue). Ann Arbor: University of Michigan Press.
BROWN, H. D., YORIO, C. A. & CRYMES, R. H. (eds) (1977). *On TESOL '77: Teaching and learning English as a Second Language: trends in research and practice*. Washington, DC: TESOL.
BROWN, R. (1973). *A first language*. London: George Allen & Unwin.
CHAUDRON, C. (1988). *Second language classrooms: research on teaching and learning*. Cambridge: Cambridge University Press.
CHOMSKY, N. (1980). *Rules and representations*. Oxford: Basil Blackwell.
CHOMSKY, N. (1981). *Lectures on government and binding*. Dordrecht: Foris.
CHRISTOPHERSEN, P. (1973). *Second language learning: myth and reality*. Harmondsworth: Penguin Educational.
COLEMAN, J. A. & TOWELL, R. (eds) (1986). *The advanced language learner. Papers from the Joint AFLS/SUFLRA Conference*. London: Centre for Information on Language Teaching.
CONNOR, U. & KAPLAN, R. B. (eds.) (1987). *Writing across languages: analysis of L2 text*. Reading, Mass.: Addison Wesley.
COOK, V. J. (1988). *Chomsky's Universal Grammar: an introduction*. Oxford: Oxford University Press.
CORDER, S. P. (1967). The significance of learners' errors. *International Review of Applied Linguistics*, 4, 161–70.
CORDER, S. P. (1971). Idiosyncratic dialects and error analysis. *International Review of Applied Linguistics*, 9, 2, 147–59.
CORDER, S. P. (1973). *Introducing applied linguistics*. Harmondsworth: Penguin Educational.
COULMAS, F. (ed.) (1981). *Conversational routine*. The Hague: Mouton.
DAVIES, A. (1989). Is international English an interlanguage? *TESOL Quarterly*, 23, 3, 447–67.
DAVIES, E. E. (1983) Error evaluation: the importance of viewpoint. *English Language Teaching Journal*, 37, 4, 304–11.
DE VILLIERS, J. C. & DE VILLIERS, P. (1978). *Language acquisition*. Harvard University Press.
DECHERT, H., & LENNON, P. (1989). Collocational blends of

advanced second language learners. In W. Oleksy (ed.), 131–68.
DICKERSON, L. J. (1975). The learner's interlanguage as a system of variable rules. *TESOL Quarterly*, **9**, 401–7.
DULAY, H., BURT, M. & KRASHEN, S. D. (1982). *Language Two*. New York: Oxford University Press.
ECKMAN, F., BELL, L. & NELSON, D. (eds.) (1984). *Universals of second language acquisition*. Rowley, Mass.: Newbury House.
ECKMAN, F. & WIRTH, J. (eds.) (1985). *Proceedings of the 12th Annual University of Milwaukee Symposium on Markedness*. New York: Plenum Press.
EDGE, J. (1989). *Mistakes and correction*. London: Longman.
ELLIS, R. (1985). *Understanding second language acquisition*. Oxford: Oxford University Press.
FAERCH, C. & KASPER, G. (eds.) (1983). *Strategies in interlanguage communication*. London: Longman.
FINE, J. (ed.) (1989). *Second language discourse: a textbook of current research*. Norwood, N.J.: Ablex.
FISIAK, J. (ed.) (1981). *Contrastive linguistics and the language teacher*. Oxford: Pergamon.
FLYNN, S. (1984). A universal in L2 acquisition based on a PBD typology. In Eckman *et al*. (eds.).
GASS, S. M. & SELINKER, L. (eds.) (1983). *Language transfer in language learning*. Rowley, Mass.: Newbury House.
GATBONTON, E. (1983). Patterned phonetic variability in second language speech: a gradual diffusion model. In B. W. Robinett & J. Schachter (eds.), 240–56.
GODARD, D. (1977) Same setting, different norms: phone call beginnings in France and the United States. *Language in Society*, **6**, 209–19.
HARTMANN, R. R. K. (1980). *Contrastive textology*. Heidelberg: Julius Groos Verlag.
HOSENFELD, C. (1977). Preliminary investigation of the reading strategies of successful and unsuccessful second language learners. *System*, **5**, 2, 110–23.
HOUSE, J. & KASPER, G. (1981). Politeness markers in English and German. In F. Coulmas (ed.).
HAWKINS, J. A. (1986). *A comparative typology of English and German: unifying the contrasts*. London: Croom Helm.
HERBERT, R. K. (1989). The ethnography of English compliments and compliment responses: a contrastive sketch. In W. Oleksy (ed.).
HINDS, J. (1983). Contrastive rhetoric: Japanese and English. *Text*, **3**, 2, 183–95.
HILLES, S. (1986). Interlanguage and the PRO-DROP parameter. *Second Language Research*, **2**, 1, 33–52.
HONEY, J. (1983). *The language trap: race, class and the 'Standard English' issue in British schools*. Kenton, Middlesex: National Council for Educational Standards.
HOUGHTON, D. & HOEY, M. (1983). Linguistics and written discourse: contrastive rhetorics. In R. B. Kaplan (ed.).
HOUSE, J. & BLUM-KULKA, S. (eds.) (1986). *Interlingual and intercultural communication: discourse and cognition in translation and second language acquisition studies*. Tübingen: Günther Narr.
HUGHES, G. A. & LASCARATU, C. (1982). Competing criteria for error gravity. *English Language Teaching Journal*, **36**, 3, 175–82.
HUGHES, G. A. & TRUDGILL, P. (1986). *Accents and dialects of English*. London: Edward Arnold.
IVIR, V. & KALOGJERA, D. (eds.) (in press). *Languages in contact and contrast: a Festschrift for Rudolf Filipovic*. Berlin: Walter de Gruyter & Co.
JAMES, CARL (1977). Judgements of error gravities. *English Language Teaching Journal*, **31**, 116–24.
JAMES, CARL (1980). *Contrastive analysis*. London: Longman.
JAMES, CARL (in press). The 'monitor model' and the role of the first language. In V. Ivir & D. Kalogjera (eds.).
JAMES, C. & GARRETT, P. (eds.) (in press). *Language awareness in the classroom*. London: Longman.

JANICKI, K. (1985). *The foreigner's language: a sociolinguistic perspective*. Oxford: Pergamon.
JENKINS, S. & HINDS, J. (1987). Business letter writing: English, French and Japanese. *TESOL Quarterly*, **21**, 2, 327–45.
JOHNSON, K. (1988). Mistake correction. *English Language Teaching Journal*, **42**, 2, 89–97.
JOHNSTONE-KOCH, B. (1983). Presentation as proof: the language of Arabic rhetoric. *Anthropological Linguistics*, **25**, 1, 47–59.
KAPLAN, R. B. (1966). Cultural thought patterns in intercultural education. *Language Learning*, **16**, 1–20.
KAPLAN, R. B. (ed.) (1983). *Annual review of applied linguistics*. Rowley, Mass.: Newbury House.
KELLERMAN, E. (1978). Giving learners a break: native language intuitions as a source of predictions about transferability. *Working Papers on Bilingualism*, **15**, 59–92.
KELLERMAN, E. (1987). Aspects of transferability in second language acquisition. Unpublished PhD thesis, University of Nijmegen.
KELLERMAN, E. & SHARWOOD SMITH, M. (eds.) (1986). *Cross-linguistic influence in second language acquisition*. Oxford: Pergamon.
KINGMAN, SIR JOHN (Chairman) (1988). *Report of the Committee of Inquiry into the Teaching of English Language: The Kingman Report*. London: HMSO for The Department of Education and Science.
KRASHEN, S. D. (1981). *Second language acquisition and second language learning*. Oxford: Pergamon.
KRASHEN, S. D. (1982). *Principles and practice in second language acquisition*. Oxford: Pergamon.
KRASHEN, S. D. (1983). Newmark's 'ignorance hypothesis' and current second language acquisition theory. In S. M. Gass & L. Selinker (eds.), 135–53.
KRASHEN, S. D. (1985). *The Input Hypothesis: issues and implications*. London: Longman.
LAUFER, B. & SIM, D. (1985). Taking the easy way out: non-use and misuse of clues in EFL reading. *English Teaching Forum*, **15**.
LENNON, P. (1989). Introspection and intentionality in advanced second language acquisition. *Language Learning*, **39**, 3, 375–96.
LENNON, P. (in press). The advanced learner at large in the L2 community: developments in spoken performance. *International Review of Applied Linguistics*, **28**.
LEVENSTON, E. A. (1978). Error analysis of free composition: the theory and the practice. *Indian Journal of Applied Linguistics*, **4**, 1, 1–11.
LEWIS, B. (1981). An essay on error. *Instructional Science*, **10**, 237–57.
LITTLEWOOD, W. T. (1981). Language variation and second language acquisition theory. *Applied Linguistics*, **2**, 2, 150–8.
LONG, M. H. (1977). Teacher feedback on learner error: mapping cognitions. In H. D. Brown, C. A. Yorio & R. H. Crymes (eds.), 278–93.
LÖRSCHER, W. (1987). On analysing translation performance. In W. Lörscher & R. Schulze (eds.), 424–40.
LÖRSCHER, W., & SCHULZE, R. (eds.) (1987). *Perspectives on language and performance: to honour Werner Hüllen*. Tübingen: Günther Narr.
NORRISH, J. (1983). *Language learners and their errors*. London: Macmillan Education.
OI, KYOKO (1986). Cross-cultural differences in rhetorical patterning: a study of Japanese and English. *JACET Bulletin*, **17**, 23–48.
OLEKSY, W. (ed.) (1989). *Contrastive pragmatics*. Amsterdam: J. Benjamins.
OSTLER, M. (1987). English in parallels: English and Arabic prose. In U. Connor & R. B. Kaplan (eds.).
PALMER, H. (1921). *Principles of language study*. Oxford: Oxford University Press.

PERERA, K. (1984). *Children's writing and reading*. Oxford: Blackwell.

PICKTHORNE, B. (1983). Error factors: a missing link between cognitive science and classroom practice? *Instructional Science*, **11**, 281–312.

POTTER, E. (1980). Miscue analysis: a cautionary note. *Journal of Research in Reading*, **3**, 2, 116–28.

PRIEST, A. G. (1981). Artificial intelligence and learning conference reports. *Instructional Science*, **10**, 277–85.

PURVES, A. C. (ed.) (1988). *Writing across languages and cultures: issues in contrastive rhetoric*. Newbury Park, Calif.: Sage Publications.

QUIRK, SIR RANDOLPH (1989). Standard English: current issues. *English Studies*, No. 2, 35–39. London: The British Council.

RICHARDS, J. C. (1971). A non-contrastive approach to error analysis. *English Language Teaching*, **25**, 204–19.

RICHARDS, J. C. (ed.) (1985). *The context of language teaching*. Cambridge: Cambridge University Press.

RICHARDS, J. C. & SUKIWIWAT, M. (1985). Cross-cultural aspects of conversational competence. In J. C. Richards (ed.).

RINGBOM, H. (1987). *The role of the first language in second language learning*. Clevedon, Avon: Multilingual Matters.

ROBINETT, B. W. & SCHACHTER, J. (eds.) (1983). *Second language learning: contrastive analysis, error analysis, and related aspects*. Ann Arbor: University of Michigan Press.

RUTHERFORD, W. E. (ed.) (1984). *Language universals and second language acquisition*. Amsterdam: John Benjamins.

SELINKER, L. (1972). Interlanguage. *International Review of Applied Linguistics*, **10**, 209–31.

SELINKER, L. & DOUGLAS, D. (1985). Wrestling with 'context' in interlanguage theory. *Applied Linguistics*, **6**, 2, 190–204.

SEY, K. A. (1974). *Ghanaian English*. London: Macmillan.

SHAUGHNESSY, M. P. (1977). *Errors and expectations*. New York: Oxford University Press.

SHIMOZAKI, M. (1988). Linkage: a contrastive study of English and Japanese. *Dokkyo University Studies in English*, **32**, 57–86.

SPOLSKY, B. (1970). Linguistics and second language pedagogy: applications or implications? *Georgetown University Round Table*, No. 22.

SUNDBY, B. & BJORGE, A. K. (1983). The codification of prescriptive grammar. *Proceedings of the 13th International Congress of Linguists, Tokyo 1982*. The Hague: CIPL, 748–51.

SWALES, J. & HASSAN, M. (eds.) (1984). *ESP in the Arab world*. Aston University: LSU.

SWAN, M. & SMITH, B. (eds.) (1987). *Learner English: a teacher's guide to interference and other problems*. Cambridge: Cambridge University Press.

TARONE, E. (1983). On the variability of interlanguage systems. *Applied Linguistics*, **4**, 2, 143–63.

TARONE, E. (1988). *Variation in interlanguage*. London: Edward Arnold.

TARONE, E., FRAUENFELDER, U. & SELINKER, L. (1976). Systematicity/variability and stability/instability in interlanguage systems. In H. D. Brown (ed.), 93–134.

TARONE, E. & PARRISH, B. (1988). Task-related variation in interlanguage: the case of articles. *Language Learning*, **38**, 1, 21–44.

TAYLOR, G. (1986). Errors and explanations. *Applied Linguistics*, **7**, 2, 144–66.

THOMAS, J. (1983). Cross-cultural pragmatic failure. *Applied Linguistics*, **4**, 2, 91–112.

URQUART, A. H. (1984). The effect of rhetorical ordering on readability. In Alderson, J. C. & Urquart, A. H. (eds.), 160–76.

VENTOLA, E. (1983). Contrasting schematic structures in service encounters. *Applied Linguistics*, **4**, 3, 242–249.

WARDHAUGH, R. (1970). The contrastive analysis hypothesis. *TESOL Quarterly*, **4**, 2, 123–30.

WENDEN, A. & RUBIN, J. (1987). *Learner strategies in language learning*. London: Prentice Hall.

WHITE, L. (1985). Markedness and parameter setting: some implications for a theory of second language acquisition. In F. Eckman, and P. Wirth (eds.)

WODE, H. (1978). Operating principles and 'universals' in L1, L2 and FLT. *IRAL*, **17**, 3, 217–231.

WOLFSON, N. (1989). The bulge: a theory of speech behaviour and social distance. In Fine, J. (ed.), 21–38.

ZOBL, H. (1986). Word order typology, lexical government, and the prediction of multiple graded effects in L2 word order, *Language*, **36**, 2, 159–83.

Language learning and teaching – theory and practice

Theory and principles

90–401 Berns, Margie. Why language teaching needs the sociolinguist. *Canadian Modern Language Review* (Toronto), **46,** 2 (1990), 339–53.

Sociolinguistics has informed language teaching theory and practice over the past 15 years or so, largely through a change of emphasis in language teaching content and innovations in materials and classroom activities. While these changes are fairly widespread and the value of insights from sociolinguistics generally is recognised, understanding of the relationship between sociolinguistics and language teaching among language teaching professionals is all too often limited to concern with language functions and ways to teach rules for use of polite forms. This paper attempts to provide a basis for a broader understanding of the potential of sociolinguistics as a resource for the language teacher, an understanding that would contribute to a language teaching theory and practice that is more responsive to the needs of learners who want to develop their ability to express, interpret, and negotiate meaning in a second language. A means of achieving this goal is offered in a consideration of a number of areas, including: the nature of language; the goals and concerns of language teaching; a sociolinguistic perspective on curriculum syllabus and materials design; the identification of appropriate goals; and the evaluation of learners' ability to use a second/foreign language.

90–402 Vivian Cook (U. of Essex). Universal Grammar theory and the classroom. *System* (Oxford), **17,** 2 (1989), 169–81.

This paper explores the implications of the principles and parameters theory of Universal Grammar for language teaching. Learning the core aspects of a second language means re-setting values for parameters according to the evidence the learner receives, perhaps starting from the L1 setting. Implications for the classroom can only be drawn for core areas of grammatical competence. Classroom acquisition depends crucially on the provision of appropriate syntactic evidence to trigger parameter-setting; certain aspects of vocabulary are also crucial. Variability, interaction, active production or comprehension, consciousness-raising and hypothesis-testing are irrelevant. Existing textbooks already supply appropriate evidence for parameter-setting; the grammatical component of syllabuses may be improved by use of principles and parameters, even if this reveals what does not need to be taught, as may the teacher's awareness of language.

90–403 Ellis, Rod. Second language learning and second language learners: growth and diversity. *TESL Canada Journal* (Montreal), **7,** 1 (1989), 74–94.

Two different traditions have grown up in the field of second language acquisition (SLA) studies. One tradition is linguistic and focuses on the process by which learners build up their linguistic knowledge of the L2, the focus being on learning. The other tradition is psychological and focuses on the different ways in which learners cope with the task of learning and using an L2. Here the focus is on the individual learner. Teachers need to take account of both these traditions; though they may appear to be in conflict, they are not, and a 'whole' approach to language teaching must consider both the structural nature of learning and the learner as an individual. Two general models of SLA which characterise much of the current research are outlined: 'development-as-sequence' and 'development-as-growth'. The development-as-sequence model claims that learners follow some kind of 'natural' route as a result of the processing complexity of different structures. It emphasises the significance of linguistic factors as determinants of acquisition. The development-as-growth model sees language development as part of the process of learning how to communicate. It attaches importance, therefore, to the changing patterns of inter-relationship of form and function. Both models are valid; they both capture important structural facts about the process of SLA.

How do learners differ in their approaches? Learning style is discussed in terms of the learner's cognitive and affective orientations to the task of learning an L2. Learners vary according to what extent they are experiential or studial on the one hand, and active or passive on the other. Do some approaches work better than others? Studies of the 'good language learner' provide a remarkably consistent picture and point to four key aspects: a concern for language form, a concern for communication, an active task approach, and awareness of the learning process.

The process of SLA is controlled by the learner. It may be possible to organise instruction to correspond to the natural sequence, but the teacher cannot tell when each learner is ready to move on. Grammar teaching should not be abandoned but teachers should be able to distinguish whether instruction is aimed at direct or indirect intervention. Indirect grammar teaching aims to raise the learner's consciousness about certain forms in the input before such forms are acquired, thereby facilitating subsequent learning. Guidelines to help teachers to encourage communication are suggested, also ways of catering for diversity in learning style (negotiating learning tasks and adapting communication to suit individual learners).

90–404 **Pennycook, Alastair** (Ontario Inst. for Studies in Ed.). The concept of method, interested knowledge, and the politics of language teaching. *TESOL Quarterly* (Washington, DC), **23**, 4 (1989), 589–618.

Examining the concept of Method in second language education, this paper argues that both a historical analysis and an investigation of its current use reveal little conceptual coherence. Ultimately, the term seems to obfuscate more than to clarify our understanding of language teaching. While this may seem at first a minor quibble over terminology, there are in fact far more serious implications. By relating the role of teaching theory to more general concerns about the production of interested knowledge and the politics of language teaching, this paper argues that Method is a prescriptive concept that articulates a positivist, progressivist, and patriarchal understanding of teaching and plays an important role in maintaining inequities between, on the one hand, predominantly male academics and, on the other, female teachers and language classrooms on the international power periphery.

90–405 **Py, Bernard** (U. of Neuchâtel, Switzerland). Les stratégies d'acquisition en situation d'interaction. [Acquisition strategies in an interactive situation.] *Français dans le Monde* (Paris), special no. Feb/Mar (1990), 81–8.

Language acquisition in a natural environment does not come about by a magical symbiosis between the learner and the target language, but rather by hard work on the part of both the learner and the native speaker. This work runs along parallel paths: the communicative (the formulation, transmission and interpretation of the message) and the metalinguistic (the resolution of communicative problems implies the organisation of fragments of the target language). Two important characteristics of asymmetrical interaction (i.e. between a learner and a native speaker) are illustrated: the desire to collaborate and the adoption of 'teacher' and 'student' roles by the native speaker and the learner respectively.

90–406 **Rampton, M. B. H.** Displacing the 'native speaker': expertise, affiliation, and inheritance. *ELT Journal* (Oxford), **44**, 2 (1990), 97–101.

The terms 'native speaker' and 'mother tongue' are criticised as being inaccurate and misleading. They emphasise the biological at the expense of the social, and confuse language as an instrument of communication with its function as a symbol of social identity. The fact that these weaknesses are exploited for political ends makes a reassessment of these assumptions particualrly important. It is thus proposed that the notion of the native speaker should be replaced by that of the 'language expert'. In that expertise is acquired, relative, and accountable, it allows for a shift of emphasis from 'who you are' to 'what you know'. The importance of language as a symbol of group identification may be expressed in the notion of language 'loyalty', of which two aspects may be distinguished: 'affiliation' and 'inheritance'. Both involve a degree of negotiation in so far as allegiance to social groups may change, as may the groups themselves; however, inheritance expresses language loyalty within social boundaries, whereas affiliation takes place across them. It is argued that the concepts introduced encourage us to consider individual cases in their wider social context, for they insist that we do not equate nationality and ethnicity with language ability and allegiance.

Language learning and teaching

90–407 **Savignon, Sandra J.** (U. of Illinois, Urbana-Champaign). Les recherches en didactique des langues étrangères et l'approche communicative. [Research in foreign language teaching and the communicative approach.] *Etudes de Linguistique Appliquée* (Paris), **77** (1990), 29–46.

A brief review of the linguistic theories and second language acquisition research that have led to the communicative approach is followed by a discussion of the inadequacies of the concept of 'functional competence' [as exemplified in the American 'Proficiency Guidelines'] as a tool for evaluating learners' competence and communicative programmes. The second half of the paper is devoted to the suggestion that a communicative course should be developed on the basis of five components: language study, the functional use of the foreign language, the language as self-expression, the language as creative expression, and the use of the language outside the classroom.

90–408 **Trim, John.** New European programmes in support of foreign language teaching. *BAAL Newsletter,* **34** (1989), 48–64.

The European Community (EC) and the Council of Europe have seen language learning as an essential aspect of closer European co-operation. The EC adopted an action programme to support foreign language teaching in 1976, but legal and political obstacles blocked its implementation. Events in the mid-1980s resuscitated interest in this area, and in 1989 the 'Lingua' programme was announced, receiving general support from member states. Its five-year budget is modest and is likely to be largely devoted to periods of residence abroad for practising teachers and university students of FLs (especially future teachers where these can be identified). The scheme is unlikely to be able to cope with the large numbers of EC English teachers eligible to study in the United Kingdom. The stimulation of the mutual study of each other's languages by smaller EC countries should, however, be considerable. One valuable result of the programme may be the development of a European unit-credit scheme, as universities become accustomed to international co-operation and mobility.

The Council of Europe works in the fields of education and culture through its Council for Cultural Co-operation (CDCC), in which 26 countries are now involved. The basic principles of the 'Council of Europe approach' to language learning/teaching, exemplified in the Threshold Level and *Un Niveau-Seuil*, gave priority to the communicative needs of learners and the definition of feasible objectives and were laid down in the early 1970s. In the early 1980s the CDCC successfully promoted the more general introduction of communicative objectives and methods in member states. Later a series of well-attended and enthusiastically received workshops for teacher trainers was held to encourage international co-operation in the implementation of these new ideas.

A new programme, *Modern language learning and teaching for European citizenship*, will extend the application of the earlier projects' findings to primary education, upper secondary education, vocational education and advanced adult education. Target themes will include the use of new technologies, bilingual education, and development of study skills. Teacher training will remain a central concern, and a series of 'new-style' workshops with organised programme of dissemination and follow-up action will be held. Co-operation with the EC in areas of common concern will be highly desirable, not least because of the CDCC's very limited funding.

Psychology of language learning

90–409 **Cameron, Lynne J.** (Coll. of Ripon and York St John, North Yorkshire). Staying within the script: personality and self-directed learning. *System* (Oxford), **18,** 1 (1990), 65–75.

A collection of case studies illustrates the reactions of overseas and British bilingual students in higher education in Britain to a procedure used to initiate a self-directed learning programme in Study Skills. This paper describes the self-assessment procedure briefly and then focuses on insights into students' feelings about learning that emerged from the trialling. Expectations and insecurity often seem to lead to the adoption, by tutors as well as by students, of particular types of roles and the playing out of 'scripts' associated with these roles. This can affect motivation and the possibility of real, effective learning taking place. In the light of this, the implications for tutors and for students of moves towards increasing the degree of self-directed learning in higher education are discussed.

90–410 Carroll, Susanne (Ontario Inst. for Studies in Ed.). Second-language acquisition and the computational paradigm. *Language Learning* (Ann Arbor, Mich), **39,** 4 (1989), 535–94.

The central claim of the cognitive science paradigm is that the mind/brain can be thought of as an information-processing device. Classical theories require explicitness about the representations in which knowledge is encoded because processes are defined as algorithms computing over them. In much current second-language acquisition (SLA) research, there is talk of 'process' and 'processing' without talk of representation or, conversely, proposals about representation with no clarity about how structures are exploited during parsing or production. To accept this state of affairs is not to take the paradigm seriously. An analysis of gender attribution in French L1 and French L2 acquisition is presented here to show how explicit models of acquisition can be developed, blending together the findings of linguistics and experimental psycholinguistics.

90–411 Ellis, Rod (Ealing Coll. of Higher Ed.). Classroom learning styles and their effect on second language acquisition: a study of two learners. *System* (Oxford), **17,** 2 (1989), 249–62.

This article reports on a study of the learning styles of two adult classroom learners of L2 German. Using data collected in a variety of ways it aims to explore to what extent and in what ways the learners' learning style varies, whether one learner's learning style results in more effective learning than the other's and the effect of the instructional style on the subjects' learning outcomes. A key distinction is made between a studial and experiential learning style. The results indicate that the two learners differed in their cognitive orientation to the learning task, that one learner might have abandoned her own preferred learning style in order to cope with the type of instruction provided and that the learning outcomes reflected what the learners set out to learn.

90–412 Gass, Susan M. (Michigan State U.). Language universals and second-language acquisition. *Language Learning* (Ann Arbor, Mich), **39,** 4 (1989), 497–534.

This paper examines the goals and assumptions of second-language acquisition (SLA) research, in particular relating these goals and assumptions to those of linguistics. It is argued that SLA *is* linguistics and that second-language data are of import in understanding the nature of language. The main focus is language universals of which three approaches (Universal Grammar, typological universals, and processing universals) are considered. Both theoretical underpinnings and empirical evidence are brought to bear in presenting supporting and disconfirming arguments for each of these three approaches. It is argued that we must take into account an understanding of how apparently disparate facts of language – which are universally related – are conceptually related before we can predict their effect on second-language acquisition. It is further pointed out that because an understanding of second-language learning necessitates an interdisciplinary approach, we must be able to specify where any single approach fits into the total picture. Finally, the author presents a view of the possible ways in which SLA and linguistics are theoretically related and points out that it is incumbent upon SLA researchers to make it known that the data they work with are of relevance and interest to the formulation of theories of language.

90–413 Giacobbe, Jorge (U. of Paris VIII, GRAL). Le recours à la langue première: une approche cognitive. [Recourse to the first language: a cognitive approach.] *Français dans le Monde* (Paris), special no. Feb/Mar (1990), 115–23.

Studies of Spanish-speaking refugees in France serve to demonstrate the strategies used by adult learners to construct for themselves an interlanguage, when they find themselves obliged to communicate but lack the linguistic resources to do so. Falling back on the forms and structures of their own language, such learners adapt and modify these, in the light of linguistic hypotheses of their own devising, so that they resemble those of the target language. Studies of pairs of languages less closely related than French and Spanish are envisaged.

90–414 **Hansen-Strain, Lynne** (Brigham Young U., Hawaii). Orality/literacy and group differences in second-language acquisition. *Language Learning* (Ann Arbor, Mich), **39,** 4 (1989), 469–96.

This paper examines group differences in second-language development from perspectives provided by the literature on orality and literacy. Findings are presented from an empirical study that investigates two hypotheses: (1) that university ESL students from traditional oral cultures tend to focus significantly more on interpersonal involvement in their ESL speaking and writing than do students from more literate cultural traditions, and (2) that in comparison with learners from more literate cultures, the learners from oral traditions tend to use difficult structures more frequently and correctly in the spoken modality than in the written. In support of both hypotheses the data indicate significant group differences in the patterning of interlanguage task variability. In conclusion, a model of discourse variability is proposed which takes into account speech modality, degree of planning, and level of interpersonal involvement.

90–415 **Krashen, Stephen** (U. of S. California). We acquire vocabulary and spelling by reading; additional evidence for the Input Hypothesis. *Modern Language Journal* (Madison, Wis), **73,** 4 (1989), 440–64.

Of the three hypotheses proposed for language acquisition, recent research is largely consistent with only one of them, the Input Hypothesis (IH). IH assumes we acquire language by understanding messages and that competence in spelling and vocabulary is most efficiently attained by reading. The Skill-building Hypothesis assumes that language is acquired through word lists, rules and exercises while the Output Hypothesis claims that language is best learned by producing it. A considerable amount of current research is reviewed and it is concluded that conscious learning does not appear to be as efficient as acquisition from input. An hour of pleasure reading is far preferable to 30 minutes of drills.

90–416 **Lennon, Paul** (U. of Birmingham). Introspection and intentionality in advanced second-language acquisition. *Language Learning* (Ann Arbor, Mich), **39,** 3 (1989), 375–96.

This paper suggests that introspective techniques can profitably be employed with the advanced learner to tap knowledge of strategic approach to the L2 acquisition task, which is largely intentional and therefore conscious. Specifically, an introspective study of four advanced learners under conditions of initial extensive exposure to the L2 community is described. Analysis is based on both written reports and interviews. A considerable degree of concurrence was found both among subjects and between the written and oral reports. This provides some confirmation for the validity of the technique and also suggests a commonness of approach among subjects to their learning task.

It was found that subjects initially adopted a strategy of listening similar to that described by Wong Fillmore (1976) for young children. Subjects' motivation was essentially to learn the language, and they did not fit into the crude classification of integratively versus instrumentally motivated learners very well.

Subjects were focused on communication rather than correctness, although they did receive limited error correction in the L2 community. Subjects tended to apply different production strategies under different circumstances and reported that their language was very much influenced by the interlocutor. They were aware of their own deficiences and mistakes, and experimented in production to seek out feedback and practice new linguistic items. Advanced learner performance would appear to be characterised by uncertainty.

Psychology of language learning

90–417 **Lepetit, Daniel** (U. of Illinois at Urbana-Champaign). Cross-linguistic influence in intonation: French/Japanese and French/English. *Language Learning* (Ann Arbor, Mich), **39,** 3 (1989), 397–413.

This article reports the findings of research on the acquisition of French intonation by native speakers of Canadian English and Japanese. Intonation is limited, in this study, to the domain of phonosyntax where intonational cues are correlated with syntactical units. Results of the study show that cross-linguistic influence in intonation is of central importance in the learner's acquisition of the target system and that one should not underestimate the degree of complexity of that influence. The study shows that it is relevant to differentiate between cross-linguistic influence of intonational phonological rules and cross-linguistic influence of phonetic characteristics, and that in both aspects a cross-linguistic influence is at work.

90–418 **Murphey, Tim** (U. of Neuchâtel, Switzerland). The song-stuck-in-my-head phenomenon: a melodic Din in the LAD? *System* (Oxford), **18,** 1 (1990), 53–64.

This hypothesis-raising article deals with the relationship between four phenomena: (1) involuntary verbal rehearsal, also called the 'Din in the head', (2) Piaget's egocentric speech, (3) Vygotsky's inner speech, and (4) the song-stuck-in-my-head (SSIMH) phenomena. The similarity of the Din to the SSIMH phenomenon is suggested based on a tentative pilot questionnaire, the database concerning the Din, a few insights from sources not yet considered in the Din literature (sports, neurology, and subvocalisation studies), and parallel phenomena in visual and kinaesthetic rehearsal. It is hypothesised that song may act as a LAD activator, or be a strategy of the LAD in the ontogenetic development of language.

90–419 **Oxford, Rebecca L.** (Pennsylvania State U.). Use of language learning strategies: a synthesis training. *System* (Oxford), **17,** 2 (1989), 235–47.

Existing research on language learning strategies is reviewed and synthesised. Good language learners use strategies in six broad groups: metacognitive, affective, social, memory, cognitive and compensatory. Good language learners manage their own learning process through *metacognitive strategies*, such as paying attention, self-evaluating, and self-monitoring. They control their emotions and attitudes through *affective strategies*, such as anxiety reduction and self-encouragement. They work with others to learn the language, using *social strategies* like asking questions and becoming culturally aware. They use *memory strategies*, such as grouping, imagery, and structured review, to get information into memory and to recall it when needed. They employ the new language directly with *cognitive strategies*, such as practising naturalistically, analysing contrastively, and summarising. Finally, they overcome knowledge limitations through *compensatory strategies*, like guessing meanings intelligently and using synonyms or other production tricks when the precise expression is unknown.

Research on what factors affect choice of language learning strategies was also reviewed. It emerged that many factors influence learning strategy choice: language being learned; duration; degree of awarenesss; age; sex; affective variables, such as attitudes, motivation level/intensity, language learning goals, motivational orientation, personality characteristics, and general personality type; learning style; aptitude; career orientation; national origin; language teaching methods; and task requirements.

Implications for strategy training are discussed. The most effective strategy training explicitly teaches learners why and how to (1) use new strategies, (2) evaluate the effectiveness of different strategies, and (3) decide when it is appropriate to transfer a given strategy to a new situation. Strategy training should be geared to learners' own needs: affective factors are especially important to consider. Factors such as national origin, sex, and course level are also crucial.

Three kinds of assessment are recommended as a guide to strategy training: (i) assessing students' current learning strategies (using techniques such as diaries, observations, interviews or surveys); (ii) determining learners' existing goals, motivations, attitudes and personality type through informal discussions or more formal assessment techniques; and (iii) considering students' language learning experience, national origin, sex, age and other background factors. These assessments do not require a great deal of effort, and certainly pay dividends in terms of more successful strategy training.

90–420 **Oxford, Rebecca** and **Crookall, David** (U. of Alabama). Research on language learning strategies: methods, findings and instructional issues. *Modern Language Journal* (Madison, Wis), **73,** 4 (1989), 404–19.

Strategies used by foreign language learners to move towards proficiency may be classified as cognitive (e.g. note taking), memory (e.g. use of mnemonics), compensation (e.g. guessing, using synonyms), communication (a misnomer for compensation strategies in speaking), metacognitive (planning one's learning), affective (e.g. self-reinforcement) and social (e.g. co-operating with peers, developing empathy). The extensive research in this area is summarised and classified according to the research methods used – introspection, interviews and thinking aloud, note taking, diary studies, surveys and factor analysis.

Language learners at all levels use strategies, but most are relatively unaware of them and do not use the full range available. On the whole, more proficient learners use a wider range of strategies in more situations. Strategy use varies with sex, ethnicity and individual personality, but it is possible and generally advisable to teach learners how and why to use, transfer and evaluate strategies.

90–421 **Palmberg, Rolf** (Åbo Akademi, Finland). What makes a word English? Swedish-speaking learners' feeling of 'Englishness'. *AILA Review* (Madrid, Spain), **6** (1989), 47–55.

'Potential' vocabulary in a foreign language consists of words not previously encountered, but which the learner can understand by making lexical inferences. 'Receptive' vocabulary consists of words which are already familiar to the learner and to which he/she can assign correct meaning. In practice, both types of vocabulary include elements of both experience and intuition. An experiment with 26 pupils (average age 14) at a Swedish-medium school in a bilingual Finnish–Swedish part of Finland was designed to find out what kind of words they recognised as English. The pupils had six years of Finnish, four years of English, and had just begun German. They were given a list of 60 words and were asked to indicate which they knew or believed to be English. Following the technique of Meara and Buxton (1987), both real and imaginary English words were included. Of these, 22 words were from the minimum basic vocabulary list recommended for 16-year-old school leavers by the Finnish National Board of General Eduction (FNBGE). Others were selected from pupil interest areas such as television and computers. The 20 non-English vocabulary items comprised imaginary, German, and Swedish words. Pupils were also asked to provide a Swedish translation of words they believed to be English.

Their success rate in identifying English words was good (86%) for FNBGE words, but dropped to 48% for non-FNBGE words. Some 18 of the test words had Swedish counterparts similar or identical in form. Ten of these were genuine cognates sharing the same meaning, and most pupils identified these correctly as English, as they did the eight deceptive cognates or 'false friends', but these elicited many incorrect translations. The pupils made quite accurate judgements on the words relating to their own interests, but were relatively unwilling to accept foreign loanwords, e.g. *anorak*, *sauna*, as English. The non-English words in the list were largely identified as such, although there was some confusion about nonsense words (e.g. *corandic*, *tarances*) sharing the physical characteristics of real English words. Some mistakes were simply the result of misreadings by individual pupils, as their attempts at translation showed. It is clear that pupils at this level possess both receptive and potential vocabularies in English, the sizes of which depend largely on the input that has been available, and on their own interests.

90–422 **Richardson, Ian M.** Discourse structure and comprehension. *System* (Oxford), **17,** 3 (1989), 339–45.

Recent discourse analysis has recommended the teaching of discourse through coherence procedure, such as conjunctions. This paper compares procedures with cohesion procedures with regard to their ease of comprehension. Suggestions are made for a model of discourse comprehension and tested experimentally. Ten different cloze procedures were constructed by the deletion of five kinds of grammatical categories. Coherence procedures were identified with nouns, verbs and conjunctions. Cohesion procedures were identified with pronouns and articles. The tests were administered to 40 Saudi EFL students and to 15 British L1 students. Inference of the deleted categories followed the same order for both groups: articles, pronouns, nouns and conjunctions. The results broadly confirmed the predictions of the model.

90–423 Schouten-van Parreren, Caroline (Free U. Amsterdam, The Netherlands). Vocabulary learning through reading: which conditions should be met when presenting words in texts? *AILA Review* (Madrid, Spain), **6** (1989), 75–84.

School methods of teaching huge numbers of words are often ineffective and demotivating. Three experimental studies are discussed (involving adults, young children and low-ability pupils respectively and performed according to the principles of action psychology, which shed light on the psychological processes involved in vocabulary learning through reading, and focus on the semantisation of new vocabulary. Arguments are put forward against presenting words in isolation and in favour of presenting them in meaningful contexts.

The first experiment concerned comprehension and retention of foreign language words presented in texts, and was meant to aid insight into the nature of the psychological processes involved in vocabulary learning through reading. The second experiment, a case study on vocabulary learning through reading picture books, aimed to gain information on textual and psychological conditions. The final experiment focused on individual differences in a variety of tasks concerning vocabulary learning and reading. Much relevant information on presenting words in texts may be gained by starting from a psychological point of view and using the method of thinking aloud.

90–424 Stone, Gregory B. (Memphis State U.) **and Rubenfield, Stepehen A.** (U. of Minnesota). Foreign languages and the business curriculum: what do the students think? *Modern Language Journal* (Madison, Wis), **73,** 4 (1989), 429–39.

A study is reported which aimed to find out what proportion of business students choose to enroll in college-level foreign language coursework, and what factors influence them in so doing. Data were collected from students enrolled in five different business schools, none of which has a recognised emphasis on international management. Results showed that only about a quarter of students had chosen to enroll in language courses. They frequently had non-business-related reasons for doing so, such as the desire to learn another language or the expectation of foreign travel. These students tended to have had positive experience of language study in high school. The difficulty for language teachers lies with the majority who have not elected to pursue language study, because they view it as more time-consuming and more difficult than other coursework, and irrelevant to their career development. Such students need to be sensitised to the relevance of international business studies and the value of foreign language skills, possibly by a campaign mounted before their junior year.

90–425 Vechter, Andrea and others. Second language retention: a summary of the issues. *Canadian Modern Language Review* (Toronto). **46,** 2 (1990), 289–303.

This short summary of an extensive annotated bibliography highlights the theoretical issues, principal studies and factors known to influence the retention of second language skills. Factors identified as relevant to changes in second language skill levels are: initially attained levels of proficiency; a supportive during- and post-training environment; exposure to other foreign languages; maturity and/or general self-awareness; literacy and/or the onset of literacy; and a perceived need to use the language after the initial training period. The notion of a 'critical skill level' which must be reached to predict/ensure retention and the effect of practice on retention are also discussed. Eleven principal research studies exploring these issues are presented in an annotated form. The article concludes with a short question/answer section. Replies in this section make reference to data reported in the annotated studies and to more recent studies in a Canadian context.

Language learning and teaching

Research methods

90–426 **Dowd, Janice** (City U. of New York) **and others.** L2 social marking: research issues. *Applied Linguistics* (Oxford), **11**, 1 (1990), 16–29.

Research on social marking in a second language (L2), with particular emphasis on pronunciation, is reviewed [examples with discussion]. Findings suggest that marking can occur at all stages of second language acquisition and in speakers of different ages, that some sounds act as markers more frequently than others; and that while several sounds marking the same social factor may shift in different directions, this may also be the case for a single sound marking several social factors. Evidence points to two levels of marking, one serving to categorise speakers on a social or biological level, the other indicating states such as beliefs and motives.

Various issues arising from this research are examined: inherent difficulties relating to the formation of hypotheses, and the analysis and interpretation of results are revealed. The necessarily large body of data and the continuous nature of speech poses problems for consistency in judgements of acceptability. Issues such as whether a group of variables constitute an entity called a 'style' and whether there is adequate rationale for the confirmation of hypotheses must be addressed if we are to recognise the effect they have on the interpretation of research results.

90–427 **Grosjean, François** (U. of Neuchâtel). Le laboratoire de traitement du language et de la parole de l'Université de Neuchâtel: recherche fondamental et appliquée. [The language and speech processing laboratory of the University of Neuchâtel: fundamental and applied research.] *Actes des Journées Suisses de Linguistique Appliquée*, I (special no. of *Bulletin CILA* (Neuchâtel)), **50** (1989), 59–65.

This article summarises the equipment and organisation of the Neuchâtel laboratory and gives examples of its work. Fundamental research in progress includes studies of the mental processes involved in perception, comprehension and production. A particular interest is the psycholinguistics of bilingualism: the authors reject explanations of bilingual behaviour in terms of two separate competences, and use a 'holistic' model which can account for code-switching. Bilinguals' behaviour in word-recognition and their pronunciation when code-switching are being investigated.

Applied research includes speech synthesis to produce a continuum between /k/ and /g/ and investigate how it is perceived, evaluation of a speech recognition system, and work on software for machine-aided translation and composition.

90–428 **Higgins, John and Wallace, Ruth** (Bristol U.). HOPALONG: a computer reading pacer. *System* (Oxford), **17**, 3 (1989), 389–99.

After reviewing some research findings about reading and reading speed, this paper describes a computer reading pacer, tentatively called HOPALONG, written at Bristol University in 1987–8. It has been subject to two sets of trials, the results of which are described below. Further trials and developments are planned. Its main purpose is to discover something about the interaction of a reader and a text by observing moment-by-moment decisions taken by the reader. It does this by running a highlight through pages of text at a speed which the reader can control with the arrow keys. It then displays a graph to show all the speed changes, and copies the complete text to the printer with inserted marks to show every point where the reader has speeded up, slowed down, paused, or re-read a page or pages. It is hoped that it can be more than just a research tool, since access to this kind of information may well be of value to teachers and to students.

Research methods

90–429 **McDonough, Jo and McDonough, Steven** (U. of Essex). What's the use of research? *ELT Journal* (Oxford), **44,** 2 (1990), 102–9.

The article is concerned with the nature and role of language teaching research, and teachers' perceptions of its relevance. A distinction is drawn between the classical 'top-down' research paradigm and the initiation of research by teachers themselves. Teachers do not always perceive the relevance of research findings to their own classrooms and teaching practices. Teachers are still seen to be recipients of information on academic research; they are concerned with processes (such as learning, classroom interaction, adaptability) whereas research insights reach them as finished products. Much academic research in applied linguistics shows unfamiliarity with the practice of language teaching.

This is not to deny that there is some 'bottom-up' research which has grown out of the ethos of teacher development and of a view of the centrality of the teacher's role. A growing trend sees the teacher in some sense as a researcher; as a starting-point for exploring teachers' perceptions of empirical research about language teaching and learning, a short questionnaire was devised and administered to 34 native English-speaking teachers of ELT. Results showed that most respondents had been, or were currently involved in research, used the product of research in their teaching, and were able to do research in their own institutions – they were, however, a highly motivated group and not a representative sample of teachers. Problems raised include the difficulty of access to much research (both conceptually and physically), and the need for teachers to receive training in how to formulate researchable questions.

90–430 **Meara, Paul** (Birkbeck Coll., London U.). Matrix models of vocabulary acquisition. *AILA Review* (Madrid, Spain), **6** (1989), 66–74.

Most tests of the effectiveness of vocabulary teaching methods are unsatisfactory because they ignore long-term changes. Given certain assumptions, the transitional probabilities of a learner forgetting a word previously remembered, or recalling a word previously forgotten, interact over time, so that the number of words remembered finally (i.e. when equilibrium is reached) is not only different from but completely independent of the number remembered initially. Whilst there are certain problems with this model, it has experimental support and would be of practical utility in standardising research. To deal with the problem of what it means to 'know' a word, a test is advocated in which subjects cross off a list of words which they 'do not know well enough to say what they mean': the list contains both target-language and nonsense words, and the test is scored by totalling crossed target words and subtracting uncrossed nonsense words.

90–431 **Mitchell, Rosamond** (U. of Southampton). Second language learning: investigating the classroom context. *System* (Oxford), **17,** 2 (1989), 195–210.

This article reviews a number of L2 classroom-based research projects, undertaken at the University of Stirling, Scotland, in which the author was involved between 1976 and 1986. The main group of projects provide accounts of foreign language teachers' instructional practices during this period, documenting shifts towards a more 'communicative' approach to foreign language teaching, but also recording teachers' continuing commitment to structural practice and the continuing use of English as a significant medium for the management of FL classrooms. A variety of research approaches were used in the course of these studies, most notably systematic observation, 'functional' analyses of classroom language, and action research; some evaluative comments are made regarding the potential and limitations of these different approaches. A later section of the article records the basic principles used in Sterling-based evaluations of L2 instructional programmes, drawing examples mainly from an evaluation study of bilingual (Gaelic–English) primary education. In conclusion, it is argued that a full understanding of classroom-based L2 learning requires the integration of sociolinguistic studies of the classroom context with psycholinguistic studies of SLA processes.

Language learning and teaching

90–432 Slimani, Assia (Inst. National d'Electricité et d'Electronique, Boumerdes, Algeria). The role of topicalisation in classroom language learning. *System* (Oxford), **17,** 2 (1989), 223–34.

The post-seventies era has seen a growing interest in the study of classroom learning processes which are believed to influence second language development. What seems to be conspicuously missing, however, are relevant research techniques capable of examining the on-going interactive processes which characterise classroom language learning.

This paper reports some of the results obtained through the implementation of an innovative technique designed to investigate the relationship between classroom interaction and learning outcomes. The paper illustrates that the detailed study of classroom interaction can explain 'uptake' – what learners claim to have learned at the end of the lesson. Topicalisation by the learners (i.e. who initiates the topics of interaction) is shown to be influential in accounting for learners' claims about uptake in one instructional setting.

Error analysis

90–433 Laufer, Batia (U. of Haifa, Israel). A factor of difficulty in vocabulary learning: deceptive transparency. *AILA Review* (Madrid, Spain), **6** (1989), 10–20.

A deceptively transparent word is one which seems to provide clues to its meaning but does not; in other words, learners think they know them but they do not. A corpus of errors collected over several years from students following courses in reading comprehension was categorised into five different categories: (1) words with a deceptively mophological structure (*outline, nevertheless, discourse*); (2) idioms (*hit and miss, sit on the fence, miss the boat*); (3) false friends (if the L2 form resembles an L1 form, the learner assumes the meaning must be the same); (4) words with multiple meanings (*since, state*); (5) 'synforms' (similar lexical forms, e.g. *cute/acute, reduce/deduce/induce*).

An experiment was carried out to verify whether deceptive transparency (DT) is a factor causing difficulty in language learning: (*a*) is the frequency of errors reduced by DT words different from the frequency of errors induced by non-DT words? (*b*) Is the learners' awareness of their ignorance of DT words different from their awareness of their ignorance of non-DT words? Subjects were 100 first-year university students of EAP. Results showed that errors were more frequent with DT words; students were less aware of their ignorance with DT words than with non-DT words; there was a significant correlation between reading comprehension and learners' awareness of unknown DT words. The presence of such words in tests of vocabulary size might interfere with the results. Errors induced by DT words could provide information about the characteristics of the L2 mental lexicon.

Testing

90–434 Arnaud, Pierre J. L. (U. Lumière-Lyon 2). Vocabulary and grammar: a multitrait-multimethod investigation. *AILA Review* (Madrid, Spain), **6** (1989), 56–65.

This article provides a brief historical overview of various approaches to testing (e.g. the development of 'communicative' techniques, etc.), maintaining that language tests serve as research instruments when proficiency is included among the experimental variables, as well as having practical functions. The author also describes previous multitrait-multimethod studies (e.g. Bachman & Palmer, 1981) which have tried to find correlations between such traits as oral production and written comprehension; the present study attempted to validate links between grammar and vocabulary tests.

Competence and proficiency are respectively defined as the integration of language components by the individual (e.g. the mental lexicon), and the degree to which an L2 speaker's performance approximates that of a native speaker in qualitative as well as quantitative terms. The author then justifies his linkage of vocabulary and grammar as aspects of pragmatic competence: some non-native speakers are able to achieve meaningful communication on the basis of their knowledge of vocabulary alone.

The two traits were assessed via three testing

methods, i.e. multiple-choice grammar items, French to English translation and error recognition, but the results [tabular data] indicated that the separate existence of vocabulary and grammar as components of L2 proficiency cannot yet be proven.

90–435 Blanche, Patrick (Cambridge English Sch., Tokyo, Japan) **and Merino, Barbara J.** (U. of California, Davis). Self-assessment of foreign-language skills: implications for teachers and researchers. *Language Learning* (Ann Arbor, Mich), **39,** 3 (1989), 313–40.

Self-assessment accuracy is a condition of learner autonomy. If students can appraise their own performance accurately enough, they will not have to depend entirely on the opinions of teachers and, at the same time, they will be able to make teachers aware of their individual learning needs. The purpose of this article is (1) to summarise the literature on self-evaluation of foreign language skills and (2) to show what it could mean to teachers and researchers. The conclusions of several self-assessment studies are somewhat contradictory, but these differences seem to support Krashen's Monitor Model/Theory. Therefore, both teachers and researchers should keep in mind that foreign language learners' self-estimates may be influenced to a varying degree by the use of the Monitor.

90–436 Dandonoli, Patricia (ACTFL) **and Henning, Grant** (Educational Testing Service). An investigation of the construct validity of the ACTFL Proficiency Guidelines and oral interview procedure. *Foreign Language Annals* (New York), **23,** 1 (1990), 11–22.

This article reports on the results of research conducted by ACTFL on the construct validity of the ACTFL Proficiency Guidelines and oral interview procedure. A multitrait-multimethod validation study formed the basis of the research design and analysis, which included tests of speaking, writing, listening and reading in French and English as a Second Language. Results from Rasch analyses are also reported. In general, the results provide strong support for the use of the Guidelines as a foundation for the development of proficiency tests and for the reliability and validity of the Oral Proficiency Interview. The paper includes a detailed description of the research methodology, instrumentation, data analyses, and results. A discussion of the results and suggestions for further research are also included.

90–437 Jonz, John (East Texas State U.). Another turn in the conversation: what does cloze measure? *TESOL Quarterly* (Washington, DC), **24,** 1 (1990), 61–83.

This study addresses a controversy in cloze testing. At issue is whether the cloze procedure measures comprehension that ranges beyond the context immediately surrounding a cloze deletion. Eight cloze passages published over the past 15 years were analysed, using a system that (*a*) estimates the quantity of text required to cue closure of any one blank and (*b*) considers the linguistic category of the deleted word. The research reported here demonstrates that across the cloze tests considered, the standard fixed-ratio cloze procedure has a high level of sensitivity to intersentential ties and lexical selections, and that the kinds of language knowledge required to complete cloze tests is virtually the same from one test to the next. The implication of these findings is that the fixed-ratio cloze procedure is far from erratic in its selection of item types. This study suggests that, for deriving tests of language comprehension, the cloze procedure produces tests that are generally consistent in the ways they measure the language knowledge of examinees.

Language learning and teaching

90–438 Matthews, Margaret. The measurement of productive skills: doubts concerning the assessment criteria of certain public examinations. *ELT Journal* (Oxford), **44,** 2 (1990), 117–21.

The currently fashionable test-type for productive skills assessment criteria expressed in terms of behavioural traits, and recently the trend has been towards the separate assessment of component sub-skills. This article points out that, from an assessor's point of view, there are serious problems relating to this particular trend and to criterion referencing in general. This problems are discussed and an alternative design is proposed. The article was prompted by experiences as an assessor for four international EFL examinations: the Royal Society of Arts Examination in the Communicative Use of English as a Foreign Languate (CUEFL); the Cambridge First Certificate in English (FCE); the Certificate of Proficiency in English (CPE); the English Language Testing Service (ELTS); and the International General Certificate of Secondary Education (IGCSE).

90–439 Pennington, Martha C. (U. of Hawaii at Manoa) **and Young, Aileen L.** (Hawaiian Missionary Academy). Approaches to faculty evaluation for ESL. *TESOL Quarterly* (Washington, DC), **23,** 4 (1989), 619–46.

On the basis of research on teacher evaluation in the larger educational context, this paper assesses the applicability to ESL of seven common faculty evaluation methods: teacher interviews, competency tests, student evaluations, student achievement, classroom observation, peer review, and faculty self-evaluation. Each method is assessed in terms of its strengths and limitations with regard to faculty evaluation in general and for TESOL in particular. A developmental orientation to faculty evaluation is outlined in which various aspects of teaching are evaluated at different stages of the teacher's career and in which a combination of methods is used. The paper concludes with a series of recommendations for the implementation of faculty evaluation in an ESL context.

90–440 Sciarone, A. G. and Schoorl, J. J. (Delft U. of Technology). The cloze test: or why small isn't always beautiful. *Language Learning* (Ann Arbor, Mich), **39,** 3 (1989), 415–38.

This article presents the findings of an experiment aimed at determining the number of blanks minimally required to ensure parallelism for cloze tests differing only in the point at which deletion starts. Two 200-item cloze tests were constructed, both based on the same Dutch text and differing only in that, in their second halves, deletion in one version lagged one word behind those in the other. The two versions were administered to two groups of 38 and 36 Indonesian learners of Dutch. Analysis of their scores on various subsets of 100, 75, and 50 items revealed that the required minimum depends upon the scoring method used. With the exact-word method, tests should contain a minimum of about 100 blanks; with the acceptable-word method, a minimum of about 75 blanks will suffice. With tests containing only 50 blanks – the number generally held to be sufficient – parallelism was found to be a matter of pure chance.

In an additional experiment, the tests involved were shown to satisfy a major requirement for the validity of any L2 proficiency tests: administration to two groups of 20 and 19 native speakers of Dutch resulted in high scores, with mean acceptable responses of 190 or more for a total of 200 items.

90–441 Wherritt, Irene and Cleary, T. Anne (U. of Iowa). A national survey of Spanish language testing for placement or outcome assessment at B.A.-granting institutions in the United States. *Foreign Language Annals,* **23,** 2 (1990), 157–65.

This research project has two principal goals for its test development: the first is to improve articulation of foreign language study between feeder high schools and the University of Iowa; the second is to create instruments to assess language competency outcomes necessary to meet the language requirement, completion of the major, and teacher certification. It was necessary to know what had been done in foreign language assessment in the United States in order not to duplicate other efforts. Information on procedures for placement or outcome assessment was difficult to find, and literature reviews and professional contacts did not locate tests that were both appropriate and affordable. A survey was undertaken on departments of Spanish language B.A.-granting institutions in the United States. Spanish language was chosen because most B.A.-granting institutions offer Spanish. Furthermore, Spanish language presents the biggest challenge in placement and assessment since large numbers of students study Spanish at both the secondary and college level. The results of the survey include information on special first-year courses, purposes for test use, tests used for freshmen placement, skills assessed, incentives and penalties for incoming freshmen, instructional activities, and class size.

Curriculum planning

90–442 **Holliday, Adrian** (Ain Shams U., Cairo). A role for soft systems methodology in ELT projects. *System* (Oxford), **18,** 1, (1990), 77–84.

There are clear uses for soft systems methodology (SSM) in ELT projects. This piece of 'technology transfer' from the field of management may help us to see better, and therefore learn to manage, some of the interpersonal problems of ELT projects, against which applied linguistics has proved less than adequate. However, there is a danger that SSM could become another example of model building taking attention away from the real world. Also, SSM can only enable an investigator to see better given an initial understanding of where problems lie. This type of understanding has been particularly difficult to achieve in many ELT projects, involved as they are with foreign cultures. Ethnographic techniques may help in achieving the understanding with which to begin; and SSM may provide a useful means for structuring ethnographic findings.

90–443 **Nunan, David** (Macquarie U., Sydney, NSW, Australia). Using learner data in curriculum development. *English for Specific Purposes* (New York), **9,** (1990), 17–32.

This paper describes an approach to curriculum development which has evolved out of a learner-centered philosophy of second and foreign language teaching. Learner-centered curricula contain similar elements and processes as those contained in traditional curricula; however, information about and from learners is incorporated into all stages in the curriculum development process. The paper takes readers through the various stages in the curriculum process, from initial needs analysis and grouping of learners through to assessment and evaluation. The use of information about and from learners for decision-making at each of these stages is illustrated with data from the Australian Adult (Im)migrant Education Programme.

Course/syllabus/materials design

90–444 **Adamson, H. D.** Prototype schemas, variation theory, and the structural syllabus. *IRAL* (Heidelberg, FRG), **28,** 1 (1990), 1–25.

The evolution of prototype theory and its implications for language teaching are surveyed in this article. A prototype is the most typical member of a category, and from this evolves the concept of the 'prototype schema', in which the elements of a class bear a family resemblance to each other, rather than having essential semantic features. This theory can be extended from semantic categories to linguistic rules. Prototype syntactic and morphological structures can be studied by means of analytical methods used by Labov in describing language variation. As far as language acquisition is concerned, research is exemplified to show that linguistic knowledge, like semantic knowledge, may be stored in prototype form, and that prototype schemas may be the precursors of categorical rules.

Recent research would seem to indicate that, while some structures [e.g. the copula] can be learned at any stage, others [e.g. word order in German] will only be learned by steps in a certain order. This has implications for functional/notional syllabuses, which have hitherto tended to disregard grading of structures, and, in particular, for a re-emergent interest in the structural syllabus.

Language learning and teaching

90–445 **John, David G.** Language isn't enough: language students and careers. *Canadian Modern Language Review* (Toronto), **46,** 3 (1990), 514–26.

When choosing fields of study, students are concerned about future careers. Research shows that the choice of subject and programme is related to perceptions of career possibilities and employability. Students who find employment easily upon graduation, especially jobs linked to their field of study, are happiest about their educational path. Humanities students, among them students of language and literature, fare badly in terms of employability in the early years after graduation, but well in the long term. Language studies must be linked to careers without sacrificing the educational core of the discipline. Results of a survey of language majors enrolled in the Applied Studies Co-op programme at the University of Waterloo show one means to link successfully language study and careers.

90–446 **Jones, Gary M.** (U. Brunei Darussalem). ESP textbooks: do they really exist? *English for Specific Purposes* (New York), **9** (1990), 89–93.

The idea of an all-embracing textbook for an ESP course is a contradiction in terms, yet the majority of ESP texts are distributed globally. The demand for them comes largely from inexperienced teachers new to ESP. Most ESP materials are an attempt to insert a specific subject content into an EFL framework, thus perpetuating a link between general EFL and ESP which should probably not exist. In many cases, ESP teachers are expected to meet an immediate demand with existing resources, hence it is hardly surprising if they resort to published material which comes fairly close to matching their learners' needs. The publishers aim primarily to sell books, even if they may not be of much use to the buyer. What the ESP teacher really needs is a bank of materials containing not only a variety of text types, but material which focuses attention on a topic and relates language practice to the topic. It would be helpful if the material in the bank could be cross referenced so that the teacher can see immediately all the uses to which it might be put. Local overseas guides might be produced suggesting how to substitute locally-relevant material where necessary. The resulting package would more closely resemble a file than a book; the user could select what was appropriate from an index and add materials of his/her own creating. The end mix should prove highly marketable and useful to all ESP practitioners.

90–447 **King, Charlotte P.** (Cumberland Coll., Kentucky). A linguistic and a cultural competence: can they live happily together? *Foreign Language Annals* (New York), **23,** 1 (1990), 65–70.

This article describes a process by which authentic documents may be integrated into first- and second-year college and high-school classes to form a cultural component in the earliest stages of foreign language study. It discusses how linguistic and cultural information may be extracted from these documents in the form of '*actes de parole*' to conform to the grammatical level of the students, and outlines ways by which cultural and linguistic information so taught may be tested.

90–448 **Legenhausen, Lienhard and Wolff, Dieter** (U. of Düsseldorf, FRG). CALL in use – use of CALL: evaluating CALL software. *System* (Oxford), **18,** 1 (1990), 1–13.

This paper is concerned with the evaluation of commercially available CALL software. In a research project the authors tested language teaching/learning programs in everyday classroom situations. The results of two of their experiments are described and assessed here. In the first part of the paper they discuss their evaluative principles and the selection of the programs evaluated. In the second part they show how they applied techniques borrowed from cognitive psychology in the evaluation of text manipulation programs of the STORYBOARD type. The results of this experiment are discussed and conclusions are drawn as to the language learning potential of this program. The last part of the paper deals with the computer simulation GRANVILLE. The authors used discourse analytical means to analyse the communicative interactions in front of the screen when students work with this program. Results indicate that GRANVILLE cannot work properly as a simulation in the foreign language classroom.

90–449 Lynch, Brian K. (U. of California, LA). A context-adaptive model for program evaluation. *TESOL Quarterly* (Washington, DC), **24**, 1 (1990), 23–42.

The literature on the evaluation of language teaching programmes has focused almost entirely on specific issues of methodology and measurement. This article presents a generalised model for ESL programme evaluation. The context-adaptive model consists of a series of seven steps designed to guide the programme evaluator through consideration of the issues, information, and design elements necessary for a thorough evaluation. These steps are illustrated with examples from the evaluation of the Reading English for Science and Technology (REST) Project at the University of Guadalajara, Mexico. The model is intended to be flexible, lending itself to effective adaptation and refinement as it is implemented in a variety of ESL/EFL contexts.

90–450 Sharp, Alastair (U. of Brunei Darussalam). Staff/student participation in course evaluation: a procedure for improving course design. *ELT Journal* (Oxford), **44**, 2 (1990), 132–7.

The limitations of testing, which is aimed at monitoring cognitive rather than affective matters, are noted; for example, the objectives/success of a course cannot easily be measured by testing mechanisms; mere percentages give little real idea of whether or not a student's needs as a language user have been met. Course evaluation must be more formative, and use a broader range of strategies (including, of course, testing itself) to check whether course objectives are reasonable or attainable. 'Illuminative' evaluation should provide such a panoramic view, being less concerned with measurement/prediction and more with description and interpretation. It might also require input from psychologists and sociologists as well as language experts.

A four month pre-sessional course for prospective undergraduates in Brunei is described, wherein the Munby (1980) needs analysis model was used. The subsequent post-course evaluation utilised such techniques as written reports from ELT staff, student questionnaires, end-of-course tests and feedback from non-ELT university lecturers (i.e. the subject-specialist instructors who later taught the course participants). Such data helped to identify problems with the course, though it was felt, for example, that collecting candidate student opinion was problematic, not least because of the culturally-determined reluctance to express forthright criticism of 'superiors'.

Teacher training

90–451 Berry, Roger (Inst. Filologii Angielskiej, Poznan, Poland). The role of language improvement in in-service teacher training: killing two birds with one stone. *System* (Oxford), **18**, 1 (1990), 97–105.

Language improvement components on training programmes for language teachers are often taken for granted, but this should not be so. Drawing on a questionnaire (which investigated teachers' needs from teacher training and influences in their teaching), the author suggests that language improvement can have a dual function: firstly, and obviously, by raising teachers' proficiency level (with everything else that this entails); secondly, and more subtly, by providing models of teaching behaviour and thereby effecting, where desired, a change in teaching practices. The tentative conclusion is that language improvement, if integrated with a methodology component, can have a central role in in-service teacher training.

Language learning and teaching

90-452 Brown, Raymond W. (Ain Shams U., Cairo). The place of beliefs and of concept formation in a language teacher training theory. *System* (Oxford), **18**, 1 (1990), 85-96.

It is accepted that a teacher's theory of teaching and learning processes evolves during his/her professional life. It is accepted also that belief systems contribute heavily to a teacher's behaviour at the levels of 'approach', 'method' and 'technique'. This paper argues that the same is true for the teacher trainer and that a danger for teacher training lies in the trainer not evolving as coherent and articulated a theory of teacher training as is possible; and that, while beliefs have their place, there is a danger of the trainer relying too heavily on them for too much of his career. It is hypothesised here that concept formation has a key role to play in teacher trainer development and action, and it is suggested that this direction has not been adequately described or followed up. An attempt is made to show how concept formation could help in developing the teacher trainer beyond a reliance on beliefs. The paper ends by hoping that controlled research will be further carried out into (*a*) the role of concepts in the development and practice of teacher training, and (*b*) the possibilities for describing and teaching the relevant concepts.

90-453 Cumming, Alister. Student teachers' conceptions of curriculum: toward an understanding of language-teacher development. *TESL Canada Journal* (Montreal), **7**, 1 (1989), 33-51.

Programmes for the education of second language teachers necessarily base themselves on conceptions of what learning to be a teacher entails. But surprisingly little study has been devoted to understanding the processes by which second language teachers actually develop their knowledge, or to defining what such knowledge consists of. This paper approaches this issue through a content analysis of data on one aspect of student teachers' professional knowledge: their conceptions of curriculum decision making. Different representations of this knowledge emerge, ranging from schemata which appear inadequately developed to those which seem sufficient to guide curriculum decision-making effectively. Implications are drawn for the education and development of second language teachers, as well as further research in this area. It is argued that current 'input-output' models of teacher education can be augmented by 'developmental learning' models, if further understanding of language teachers' professional knowledge is obtained.

90-454 Woodward, Tessa (Hilderstone Coll. and Pilgrims Language Courses, Kent). An analysis of current approaches to process in teacher training for EFL as evidenced by teacher training manuals. *System* (Oxford), **17**, 3 (1989), 401-8.

This article surveys 10 current EFL teacher-training books [tabular data]. The major aim of the analysis was to focus on the ways in which these books handled the learning process itself, since they were primarily meant for self-access situations, where there is no intermediary course tutor or teacher trainer. Most of the TEFL books considered seem to assume that content was all important, and that readers will already possess the study skills and strategies necessary to digest, recall and use the information presented; i.e. process was somehow to take care of itself.

In basic terms, two types of self-access/process clues were found: (1) pre-reading exercises and (2) 'moving on' exercises that presume the reader has grappled with and understood (but not actively worked with) the content. It was also perceived, though, that books which have ample process suggestions also assume a privileged and adept professional reader with wide access to colleagues, classes, other books/journals, etc.) In basic terms, there are few authors who feel that the TEFL book alone is probably inadequate, and even fewer who see readers as individuals with different learning styles.

Teaching methods

90–455 Arndt, Horst and others. Überlegungen zu Sprachprogrammen für Manager in Industrie und Handel. [Aspects of language programmes for managers in industry and business.] *Die Neueren Sprachen* (Frankfurt am Main, FRG), **89,** 1 (1990), 2–19.

Foreign-language teaching geared to upper-level management in trade and industry seems to be a relatively neglected aspect of specialised, career-oriented foreign language teaching as a whole. The specific kind of communication and foreign-language skills required by managers are analysed with the institutional framework of inhouse foreign-language training in mind. Specialised language training is less important for managers than strategies of interaction that will enable them to perform their tasks in international negotiations.

90–456 Bahns, Jens. Consultant not initiator: the role of the applied SLA researcher. *ELT Journal* (Oxford), **44,** 2 (1990), 110–16.

This article examines some possible relationships between research in second language acquisition (SLA) and foreign language teaching. Special reference is made to research findings in SLA about the 'order of acquisition' of grammatical items, and to a model of application for such findings to classroom practice. The model proposed that, for practising teachers, SLA findings about the order of acquisition of grammatical items are best seen as data to be consulted when appropriate, rather than as information which should by itself be used to initiate change.

90–457 Carrell, Patricia L. (U. of Akron) **and others.** Metacognitive strategy training for ESL reading. *TESOL Quarterly* (Washington, DC), **23,** 4 (1989), 647–78.

Recent research in second language reading has focused on metacognition (literally, cognition of cognition). These studies investigate metacognitive awareness of reading strategies and the relationships among perception of strategies, strategy use, and reading comprehension. Strategy research suggests that less competent learners may improve their skills through training in strategies evidenced by more successful learners. Relatively little research on metacognitive strategy training has been done in a second language context or, more specifically, in second language reading.

This article reports a study of metacognitive strategy training for reading in ESL. Strategy training was provided to experimental groups. Control groups received no strategy training, but participated in pre- and post-testing. Several research questions are addressed: does metacognitive strategy training enhance L2 reading? If so, does one type of strategy training facilitate L2 reading better than another? How is the effectiveness of metacognitive strategy training related to the learning styles of the students? Results show that metacognitive strategy training is effective in enhancing second language reading, and that the effectiveness of one type of training versus another may depend upon the way reading is measured. Further, the results show that the effectiveness of the training is related to differences in the learning styles of the students.

90–458 de Kock, Josse. De la enseñanza de las lenguas extranjeras. [On teaching foreign languages.] *Revista de la AEPE* (Madrid), **36/7** (1989), 9–18.

Mastery of a foreign language calls for linguistic awareness which in turn demands study of grammar, but of grammar in a living context, not the rigid application of stereotyped rules. Students at university level should study non-literary texts and texts by modern authors which have been chosen for their linguistic potential in exploiting the possibilities and resources of the language, and not for their supposed literary merits; students should be led to analyse and reflect upon the inner logic and underlying coherence of their target language.

An invaluable aid to learning, an index of the relative frequency of grammatical forms, can be established by the students themselves, making use of the computer.

Language learning and teaching

90–459 Dollerup, Cay and others. Vocabularies in the reading process. *AILA Review* (Madrid, Spain), **6** (1989), 21–33.

Using a study of Danish freshman undergraduates' vocabularies as a springboard, the paper explores and discusses a number of current assumptions about vocabularies in the mother tongue and in foreign language teaching. The conclusion is that as far as reading is concerned, a reader's vocabulary is part of the process of reading: it is a function of the texts and its contents, of the reader's reading strategies, and of the reader's more or less stable 'word knowledge'. In the reading of a specific text there is a constant interplay between these factors which suggest that a vocabulary in reading is 'fluid'. Pedagogically, this theory implies that there should be a deliberate teaching of reading strategies in addition to other methods.

90–460 Haastrup, Kirsten (Copenhagen Business School). The learner as word processor. *AILA Review* (Madrid, Spain), **6** (1989), 34–46.

Teachers should be concerned about raising students' awareness level of communication and learning. Students need to know more about perceived similarity and transfer possibilities as well as about top-ruled and bottom-ruled processing as potentially effective or ineffective inferencing procedures. Getting to understand the dynamic and interactive nature of language processing is a difficult task. Moreover, as for vocabulary learning based on written input, it seems likely that in order to be a good processor of text and of words the student must also be a good reader in both the L1 and L2. An additional requirement is knowledge of the world, both general and L2-specific. If a student is to be a competent word processor, s/he must also be a good text processor and world processor.

90–461 Hafiz, F. M. and Tudor, I. (Free U. of Brussels, Belgium). Graded readers as an input medium in L2 learning. *System* (Oxford), **18**, 1 (1990), 31–42.

The article describes an experiment into the effect of a 90-hour extensive reading programme using graded readers on the language development of a group ($N = 25$) of learners of English as an L2 in Pakistan. Results show significant gains in both fluency and accuracy of expression, though not in range of structures used. It is suggested that extensive reading can provide learners with a set of linguistic models which may then, by a process of over-learning, be assimilated and incorporated into learners' active L2 repertoire. The results are discussed with reference to a related study by the same authors in an ESL context in the UK.

90–462 Horowitz, Daniel (International Christian U., Tokyo, Japan). The undergraduate research paper: where research and writing meet. *System* (Oxford), **17**, 3 (1989), 347–57.

Research and writing are both recursive processes. Researchers begin by asking questions, then search for answers, sometimes find them, and in the finding (or not finding) discover new questions to be answered. Writers move in a similar cyclical pattern, from planning what they will write, to composing, to evaluating what they have written and then back again to making new plans for revising their work. Common procedure for the teaching of undergraduate research paper writing separates these processes into two distinct stages, research followed by writing, but this paper argues that there is much to be gained by encouraging their interaction from the very beginning. The process of research writing is followed from the choosing of topics to evaluation of the final product, and activities are suggested which encourage students to see research writing as the ongoing search for better questions, better answers, and better ways to communicate those answers.

Teaching methods

90–463 Jungblut, Gertrud. 'How to call a spade a spade'. Begründungen für monolinguale Wortbedeutungsvermittlung im Fremdsprachenunterricht. [In defence of monolingual aids to understanding vocabulary in foreign language learning.] *Die Neueren Sprachen* (Frankfurt am Main, FRG), **89,** 1 (1990), 55–68.

Although the monolingual approach has been practised with success for years now, it is repeatedly questioned by critics who point to a lack of theory to support it. In this article an attempt is made to show that there are scientific theories which can be cited to justify this teaching concept. Both general semiotics and the findings of neurophysiological research indicate that learning a language takes the form of a 'semiotic cycle', in which the learners are (supposed to be) rendered capable of activating concepts in response to the stimuli from the things and events of the real world (their environment), concepts that are linked to the meaning of a word from the sounds of the word in a foreign language. Thus, in the majority of cases learning a foreign language entails a process of acculturation which takes place within the immediate context of sensory perception.

90–464 Lund, Randal J. (Brigham Young U., Provo, Utah). A taxonomy for teaching second language listening. *Foreign Language Annals,* **23,** 2 (1990), 105–15.

This article describes a taxonomy of real-world listening tasks as a conceptual framework for teaching listening. The key elements of the taxonomy are listener function and listener response. In listening, function is defined as 'the aspects of the message the listener attempts to process'. The six functions significant for second language teaching are identification, orientation, main idea comprehension, detail comprehension, full comprehension, and replication. Listener response is also a key feature of any listening task. Nine categories are described. Function and response can be selected independently of each other, as suggested by the function-response matrix, allowing for wide variation in task difficulty for any given text.

The implications of the taxonomy for the design of listening instruction and the selection of authentic texts are discussed. The taxonomy suggests that growth in listening proficiency is a process of expanding to new function and response categories in familiar contexts. The many options in the taxonomy enable one to structure effective listening tasks involving authentic texts even at novice levels.

90–465 Motteram, Gary J. (U. of Manchester). Using a standard authoring package to teach effective reading skills. *System* (Oxford), **18,** 1 (1990), 15–21.

This article discusses the way in which one particular piece of computer software can be used to teach the skill of reading. The software has not been designed specifically for this end, but can be used to teach any subject area. The software is of the authoring type which means that any teacher willing to spend a few hours becoming proficient in its use can make effective, interesting and useful teaching material. These materials have proved motivating and valid at a variety of levels and with different types of students.

90–466 Murtagh, Lelia (Linguistics Inst. of Ireland, Dublin). Reading in a second or foreign language: models, processes, and pedagogy. *Language, Culture and Curriculum* (Clevedon, Avon), **2,** 2 (1989), 91–105.

Current research on reading in a second or foreign language is reviewed. Good L2 reading is characterised by fast, automatic word recognition which releases more time for the use of syntactic and contextual information. Successful readers also make good use of background information. Many strategies for L2 reading are generalised from L1 reading, but the degree of successful transfer is limited by the learner's overall proficiency in L2. Research provides no decisive answers to the issue of correct sequencing of L1 and L2 reading instruction, and suggests that findings will have to be interpreted in the light of the socio-economic, linguistic, and cultural context. The integration of top-down and bottom-up strategies is also a feature of good L2 reading. Overall, L2 reading instruction should focus on the construction of meaning jointly from the reader's own background information and the new information contained in the text. Simplified texts should not be used unless the readers still have basic problems with specific syntactic contrasts.

90–467 **Olsen, Leslie A.** (U. of Michigan) **and Huckin, Thomas N.** (U. of Utah). Point-driven understanding in engineering lecture comprehension. *English for Specific Purposes* (New York), **9** (1990), 33–47.

Non-native speakers have long been known to have trouble understanding academic lectures. ESP researchers and teachers agree that the problem lies mainly at the discourse level, not at the sentence level; accordingly, a body of discourse-oriented teaching materials for lecture comprehension is now on the market. Though a step in the right direction, these materials fail to do justice to the rhetorical, strategic nature of academic lectures. As this study shows, students may understand all the words of a lecture (including lexical connectives and other discourse markers) and yet fail to understand the lecturer's main points or logical argument.

This study was an exploratory one. Fourteen NNS graduate and undergraduate students watched an authentic 16-minute videotaped lecture on a topic in mechanical engineering and then were asked to provide immediate-recall summaries which were then analysed in consultation with the lecturer. Although the lecture was clearly structured around several main points, most of the students failed to grasp these points. These results are discussed in terms of listening strategies: the successful students used a 'point-driven' strategy while the unsuccessful ones used an 'information-driven' strategy. It is concluded that students should be taught how to listen to lectures in a more rhetorical, strategic way. More generally, if we are to teach students to understand and communicate more effectively, we should help them see how the organisation of their discourse fits into the large goals, agendas, and contexts in their fields.

90–468 **Orban, Clara and McLean, Alice Musick.** A working model for videocamera use in the foreign language classroom. *French Review* (Baltimore, Md), **63,** 4 (1990), 652–63.

The authors offer a working model of exercises and practical suggestions for videocamera use with foreign-language students of all abilities and levels. Self-evaluation is central. The model involves videotape recording of students under supervision. Equipment and techniques are discussed, the sequence of exercises in the model is reviewed, and grading, staff co-operation and technical considerations are addressed. The exercises are grouped into three categories: (*a*) text-supported speech, (*b*) speech supported by a (near)-native interlocutor, and (*c*) speech without external support.

With video, the configuration of facial muscles during the production of particular phonemes can be better demonstrated. Videocamera self-evaluation allows for necessary individualised attention. It concentrates primarily on phonetics, but also reinforces grammatical structures and heightens the student's awareness of communicative strategies in order to improve overall communicability. Group dynamics play a key role. [Examples of exercises of each type.] Video may be seen as gimmicky if its pedagogic usefulness is not explicitly detailed. Oral ability can best be monitored through video, and students have tangible proof of how well they speak and how their language skills can improve with time and effort.

90–469 **Puren, Christian** (U. of Bordeaux III). Méthodes d'enseignement, méthodes d'apprentissage et activités metaméthodologiques en classe de langue. [Teaching methods, learning methods and metamethodological activities in language classes.] *Langues Modernes* (Paris), **84,** 1 (1990), 57–70.

The differences between language learning and language acquisition as defined by Krashen and others are confounded by adherents to the communicative approach, who set up principles and methods of teaching while at the same time stressing the importance of acquisition to achieve the goals of learning. One way to escape this confusion is to introduce 'metamethodologies' into classes whereby different teaching and different learning methodologies can be discussed in order to reach agreement on an approach acceptable to all. A typology of learning activities is proposed and discussed, underlying which is the notion that if teachers are responsible for their teaching, learners must also take responsibility for their learning.

90–470 Rose, Sheila D. Cultural studies and multiculturalism: an experiment in classroom twinning. *Language, Culture and Curriculum* (Clevedon, Avon), **2,** 2 (1989), 117–33.

Students aged 9–12 in three West Hartford, Connecticut classrooms were engaged in a four-month study about themselves, their community and the interdependence of cultures worldwide. Each classroom was twinned with a classroom in Canada (Inuit), England or Spain, and an ongoing exchange of letters, projects and reports took place. The study sought to determine (1) whether this type of contact results in a clearer and more sensitive understanding by American students of their own community, and its similarities and interdependence with another community in the world; (2) whether more sensitive or empathetic understanding, if it occurs, is transferred to other foreign people not involved in the study; and (3) whether the skills of mutual goal setting and co-operative learning were more fully developed as a result of participation in the twinning study. Students were given pre- and post-tests on a variety of instruments: open-end questions, picture-drawing, interview, and essay. The use of these projective measures in the assessment of social studies programmes is explained and illustrated. Results showed that cultural studies with broad objectives have to confront high levels of ethnocentrism. Yet there were clear indications that progress towards multiculturalism can be made using the school twinning technique.

90–471 Shaffer, Constance (Hun Sch. of Princetown). A comparison of inductive and deductive approaches to teaching foreign languages. *Modern Language Journal* (Madison, Wis), **73,** 4 (1989), 395–403.

An investigation was carried out to determine whether high school foreign language students' understanding of grammatical concepts and their linguistic performance were better served by inductive or deductive approaches. An inductive approach is one in which students formulate the grammatical rule for themselves. A deductive approach is one in which the rule is given first. Some 319 students in three high schools learned when to use one of four structures in French and Spanish. Of these, 159 were given an inductive approach and 160 a deductive one. No significant difference was found between the mean scores for either group. However, there was a trend in favour of inductive approaches, not least because they tend to promote active participation by learners and involve them in discovering rules by themselves rather than merely being told by teachers.

90–472 Tudor, Ian (Inst. de Phonétique, Brussels, Belgium). Pre-reading: a categorisation of formats. *System* (Oxford), **17,** 3, (1989), 323–38.

The article briefly surveys the importance of background knowledge in L2 reading comprehension and discusses the role of pre-reading within this context. On this basis, a categorisation of pre-reading formats occurring in a corpus of ELT materials is proposed, each of the seven formats identified being discussed and exemplified with reference to the initial theoretical survey. In conclusion a few general guidelines for the use of pre-reading are suggested.

90–473 van der Vyver, Dawid H. and Botha, H. Ludolph. The implementation and evaluation of suggestopedic/SALT language teaching in South Africa since 1984. *Per Linguam* (Stellenbosch, South Africa), **5,** 2 (1989), 21–59.

The article is an extract from a comprehensive report and gives an overview of the development of suggestopedic/SALT language teaching in South Africa. First the theoretical framework, objectives and methodology of the approach are given, followed by reports on SALT conferences. Various projects are described, especially the launching of a pilot project to upgrade English in education for blacks in KwaZulu by the Interuniversity Committee for Language Teaching. How this led to the establishment of the UPTTRAIL Trust and the engagement of the Institute for Language Teaching at the University of Stellenbosch, in cooperation with the HSRC, to work out a research design for the pilot project is explained.

90–474 **Vila, Joaquin** (Illinois State U.) **and Pearson, Lon** (U. of Missouri, Rolla). A computerised phonetics instructor: Babel. *CALICO Journal* (Provo, Utah), **7,** 3 (1990), 3–29.

Babel is an expert system able to animate (graphically) and reproduce (acoustically) a text in any language which uses the Latin alphabet. This system has been developed to aid language learners and to help instructors teach the fine nuances of phonemes. Each phoneme has a unique sound and thus requires a precise positioning of the vocal organs which are displayed on the screen in two different projections: a front view and a profile cross view of a human face in synchronisation with the output sounds of the speech synthesiser.

Teaching particular languages

English

90–475 Adamson, H. D. (U. of Arizona). ESL Students' use of academic skills in content courses. *English for Specific Purposes* (New York), **9** (1990), 67–87.

The recent emphasis on content-based ESL instruction is motivated by research showing that English proficiency does not correlate with academic success. Case studies of fifteen ESL students in content classes with native English speakers suggest that one reason for this lack of success is that the ESL students lack effective academic skills. The students in the case studies showed a wide variety of strategies for taking notes, reading, using dictionaries, speaking in class, and personal organisation. Both effective and ineffective strategies were used. When the students were given assignments for which they lacked adequate background knowledge or academic skills, they adopted coping strategies for completing their assignments without fully understanding the material. The case studies suggest that academic skills are best taught in connection with authentic content material, so an experimental pre-course was set up in which college students in a theme-based ESL course attended an undergraduate linguistics course for three weeks. An analysis of the students' quizzes, papers, and other materials suggests that such a course is an effective way to teach academic skills.

90–476 Assbeck, Johann. Von der Textarbeit zur literarischen Analyse: Thesen und Vorschläge für die Drameninterpretation in der 11. Klasse am Beispiel von LeRoi Jones' 'A Black Mass'. [From work on text, to literary analysis: arguments and suggestions for dramatic interpretation in secondary stage I, taking as an example LeRoi Jones' 'A Black Mass'.] *Die Neueren Sprachen* (Frankfurt am Main, FRG), **89,** 1 (1990), 20–38.

The teaching of English literature in advanced level classes has in many cases been reduced to a mere application of academic methods of literary analysis. This article suggests that students should be introduced to literary analysis by focusing on 'words', i.e. by analysing the ambivalent meanings, the collocations and connotations of the important words, thus drawing on the student's specific experience as a language learner. The main objective is to make students aware of the complexity of literary language and to enable them to move from a basic understanding of the text towards critical evaluation without totally depending on guidance from the teacher.

90–477 Bensoussan, Marsha (Haifa U., Israel). EFL reading as seen through translation and discourse analysis: narrative vs. expository texts. *English for Specific Purposes* (New York), **9** (1990), 49–66.

Though in some respects easier than expository texts, narrative texts can pose special problems for foreign language learners. Such differences can be examined in terms of the macro- and microlevels of propositional content, communicative functions, vocabulary, verb tenses, parts of speech, pronoun agreement, and grammatical cohesion. Learners reading expository texts are expected to follow a logical argument (with explanations, contrasts, cause/effect, etc.) usually organised with typical markers of cohesion. Readers of narrative texts may need to follow dialogues characterised by description, irony, subtle nuances, and double entendres.

This paper examines reading problems by means of discourse analysis of students' translations. It is based on two previous experiments in which first-year university students translated English texts into their native language, Hebrew or Arabic. For both text types, learners had difficulty with propositional content, vocabulary, and pronoun agreement. Communicative function appeared to cause difficulty in the narrative but not the expository text. Grammatical cohesion, in contrast, proved difficult in the expository but not the narrative text.

Teaching particular languages

90–478 **Bourne, Jill** (NFER, Slough, Berks). Local authority provision for bilingual pupils: 'ESL', bilingual support and community languages teaching. *Educational Research* (Windsor, Berks), **32,** 1 (1990), 3–13.

This paper outlines the findings of a national survey conducted between 1985 and 1988 into local authority provision for language support for the curriculum learning of bilingual pupils, and for the teaching of the languages of local linguistic minority groups in the schools of England and Wales. The full report, *Moving into the Mainstream: LEA Provision for Bilingual Pupils*, was published in the autumn (Bourne, 1989).

By 1987, although provision for bilingual pupils in England was still seen largely in terms of the need for English language support, greater emphasis was being given to support for effective curriculum learning either through English or through pupils' other languages, where this was possible. A significant increase in provision for the teaching of pupils' languages other than English within the school curriculum had also taken place, boosted by the extra funding available prior to 1987 through 'Section 11'.

Constraints on the further development of provision for bilingual pupils which were identified were: (1) The absence of clear structures for consultation with minority linguistic groups at national and local levels on appropriate provision. (2) The absence of forceful policy and funding targeted at teacher training institutions to increase the admission and training of bilingual teachers as language specialists and on mainstream subject courses. (3) The absence of explicitly targeted national in-service priority funding for helping schools to respond to bilingualism effectively. (4) The absence of any central curriculum and materials development body for bilingualism and community languages. (5) The expectation among most LEAs that any provision made for bilingual pupils should be supported by extra, special funding. (6) The lack of clarity in Home Office 'Section 11' regulations for funding, and the absence of any more appropriate source of funding for educational provision specifically to meet the needs of minority linguistic groups in England. (7) The paucity of widely available documented models of good practice in adapting mainstream provision for multilingual classrooms, and of models of practice for community languages teaching in mixed first and second language classrooms.

90–479 **Chambers, Fred** (West Sussex Inst. of Higher Ed.) **and Erith, Philip** (U. of Benin, Lome, W. Africa). On justifying and evaluating aid-based ELT. *ELT Journal* (Oxford), **44,** 2 (1990), 138–43.

The objective justification of aid-based ELT programmes is made difficult by inherent problems of evaluation. Commercially-inspired ELT programmes either make a profit and are justified, or fail, but aid-based ELT is not designed primarily to make a profit. ELT programmes are, rightly, in competition for scarce funds with all other forms of aid, educational or non-educational. The ultimate objective of any ELT aid programme as far as the recipient nation is concerned is adequate command of English to ensure access to world science, commerce and industry, to be achieved by a process that begins with improving ELT in institutes of learning. The question of whether a nation actually does prosper by this process is virtually impossible to answer. In spite of this, aid-based ELT programmes continue to exist because both donor and host judge them to be of value; because they are often perceived (mistakenly) by the host as 'something for nothing'; and because English is such a dominant world language that there is no rational alternative.

In future it may be necessary to review the existing paradigm of ELT programmes, and to create a role for ELT as a vehicle for some more general set of objectives, such as making it the medium for imparting important subject matter, e.g. healthcare. One inherent problem in this approach is that language programmes could risk failing to communicate crucial information adequately. A safer option is to use ELT to provide practice in some useful educational techniques, as in the Primary Project in Singapore, concerned with improving ELT methodology in primary schools. The Sabah Rural Primary Education Programme in Malaysia combines ELT with the development of an INSET network, establishing in rural areas groups of teachers meeting regularly with a coordinator to develop and practise suitable teaching techniques with materials. In such initiatives, evaluation of the ELT element need no longer be the sole arbiter of success. Conversely, in future any ELT programme without parallel educational objectives will face stiffer demands to justify its existence.

English

90–480 **Hall, Chris** (Wright State U.). Managing the complexity of revising across languages. *TESOL Quarterly* (Washington, DC), **24,** 1 (1990), 43–60.

Although previous research in ESL composition suggests a link between writing in a first and second language, few studies have investigated this relationship in the context of the revising process. This article examines revision in controlled L1 and L2 writing tasks. Four advanced ESL writers with differing first language backgrounds, wrote two argumentative essays in their native languages and two in English. Revisions were then analysed for specific discourse and linguistic features. The results, for the most part, indicate striking similarities across languages. However, some differences are noted, suggesting that while proficient writers are capable of transferring their revision processes across languages, they are also capable of adapting some of those processes to new problems imposed by a second language.

90–481 **Laufer, Batia** (U. of Haifa). Ease and difficulty in vocabulary learning: some teaching implications. *Foreign Language Annals* (New York), **23,** 2 (1990), 147–55.

This paper discusses the relationship between ease/difficulty in learning particular words and some issues in the teaching of vocabulary. Some factors that interfere with learning a word are the following: similarity of form between the word and other words (*embrace/embarrass, price/prize*); morphological similarity between it and other words (*industrial/industrious, respectable/respective*); deceptive morphological structure (*infallible*); different syntactic patterning in L1; differences in the classification of experience between L1 and L2 (one-to-many correspondence, partial overlap in meaning, metaphorical extension, lexical voids, multiplicity of meaning); abstractness; specificity; negative value; connotations non-existent in L1; differences in the pragmatic meaning of near synonyms and of L1 translation equivalents; the learning burden of synonyms; the apparent rulelessness of collocations.

Word learnability (ease/difficulty in learning a particular word) can serve as a guideline to the following: the selection of words to be taught; their presentation (quantity, grouping, language of presentation, isolation/context issue); the facilitation of long-term memorisation (meaningful tasks, mnemonic techniques, rote learning, reactivation); the development of strategies for self-learning; and the assessment of vocabulary knowledge.

90–482 **Nation, Paul** (Victoria U. of Wellington, New Zealand). Improving speaking fluency. *System* (Oxford), **17,** 3 (1989), 377–84.

This paper examines the improvement of learners of English during the performance of a speaking activity which involves repeating the same unrehearsed talk. Improvements in fluency, grammatical accuracy, and control of the content showed that during the short time spent doing the activity, learners performed at a level above their normal level of performance. It is argued that working at this higher than usual performance is a way of bringing about long-term improvement in fluency.

90–483 **Olshtain, Elite and Cohen, Andrew.** The learning of complex speech act behaviour. *TESL Canada Journal* (Montreal), **7,** 2 (1990), 45–65.

The study reported in this article concerns itself with the learning and teaching of the more subtle and complex features of the speech act of apology in English. Based on the current knowledge on apology speech act behaviour, the authors addressed questions relating to the efficacy of teaching such elements as: choice of semantic formula; appropriate length of realisation patterns; use of intensifiers; judgement of appropriacy and students' preferences for certain teaching techniques. In order to attempt to answer these questions a training study was carried out with 18 adult Hebrew-speaking learners of English. The study consisted of: (*a*) a pre-teaching questionnaire aimed at assessing the subjects' use of apologies; (*b*) a teaching materials packet covering three classroom sessions and (*c*) a post-teaching questionnaire. The findings suggest that although there is no clear-cut quantitative improvement of the learners' speech act behaviour after the given training programme, there is an obvious qualitative approximation of native-like speech act behaviour with respect to types of intensification and downgrading, choice of strategy and awareness of situational factors. It seems,

Teaching particular languages

therefore, that the teaching of speech act behaviour is a worthwhile project even if the aim is only to raise the learners' awareness of appropriate speech act behaviour.

90–484 Paper, Li Chuang. An ESL motivations assessment for a community-based ESL programme. *TESL Canada Journal* (Montreal), **7,** 2 (1990), 31–44.

This paper concerns an ESL motivations assessment of adult Chinese learners at Chinese Information and Community Services (CICS). Some 512 ESL learners participated in the survey. The findings of the survey are as follows: (1) The motives of adult Chinese immigrants attending ESL classes include linguistic needs, basic skills, cultural awareness, social interaction, and writing resumés. (2) There are no significant differences in perceived motivations according to age, education level, and length of stay in Canada; however, there are slight differences among a few indicators. (3) The implications for ESL teaching are that (a) teaching objectives should include both the teaching of English and Canadian culture; (b) the teaching of English should focus on language needed for conducting everyday life and social interaction; (c) all four language skills (speaking, listening, reading, and writing) should be taught at the same time with more emphasis on the first three skills; (d) pronunciation and vocabulary teaching is also necessary.

90–485 Schleppegrell, Mary and Royster, Linda. Business English: an international survey. *English for Specific Purposes* (New York), **9** (1990), 3–16.

This paper reports the results of an evaluation of 55 English language training (ELT) schools in Europe, Asia, the Middle East, and Central and South America. Course objectives, instructional approaches and materials, classroom activities, staff qualifications, and administrative procedures were evaluated to determine each school's ability to provide quality training for business professionals. The schools were classified as one of three types: world-wide commercial, small and midsized commercial, and academic/governmental. The quality of training provided by each type of school varied widely. The survey indicates that most schools offering ELT programmes for business people do not use business-oriented instructional materials or have clear instructional goals. Only half of the schools surveyed employed certified instructors and used business-related activities in their classes. Most schools had adequate administrative procedures. Some regional differences were also found in the extent to which programmes met the evaluation criteria used in this survey.

90–486 Side, Richard (Eckersley Sch. of English, Oxford). Phrasal verbs: sorting them out. *ELT Journal* (Oxford), **44,** 2 (1990), 144–52.

Phrasal verbs create special problems for students, partly because there are so many of them, but also because the combination of verb and particle so often seems completely random. Students' ability to understand and use phrasal verbs is heavily influenced by their knowledge of their own language, and interference from that language. The problem is that interference is not merely linguistic, but conceptual. Concepts like *up* and *down, to* and *from*, are culturally variable. The particle is integral to the meaning of the phrasal verb and in some cases carries more weight of meaning than the verb, but in other examples, e.g. *You can hang your coat up here*, it adds little to the communicative value of the verb. The meaning of the adverbial particle is not always synonymous with the corresponding preposition, thus *put up with* has nothing to do with upward movement. Such highly idiomatic examples fitting no category are, fortunately, rare. Learners are, however, not helped by the patchy treatment of phrasal verbs in many dictionaries.

If one looks closely at the particle, patterns emerge which suggest that the combinations are not so random after all. A more flexible approach to the relationships between phrasal verbs enables the outline of a system to establish itself. By thinking laterally, metaphorically, and even pictorially, teachers can arrange phrasal verbs into related, more learnable categories. The analogous nature of these verbs means that single examples should not be taught in isolation. Connections should always be made to establish their context within the language, to show they are meaningfully idiomatic rather than meaninglessly random. This often means grouping phrasal verbs together according to the particle rather than the verb. There must be a balance between presenting phrasal verbs in their context within a text, and presenting them in their overall linguistic context, i.e. in lists. Much profitable discussion can arise from students making a decision to assign a particular phrasal verb to one or other category of particle, especially with ambiguous examples. Students' own efforts to create meaningful patterns are in themselves aids to memory.

90–487 Spada, Nina and Lightbown, Patsy M. Intensive ESL programmes in Quebec primary schools. *TESL Canada Journal* (Montreal), **7,** 1 (1989), 11–32.

This paper is a report on a study designed to investigate the second language development of francophone children in experimental intensive ESL programmes in Quebec primary schools. Classroom interaction patterns and learners' contact with and attitudes toward English were also investigated. Learners in the intensive programmes were compared with learners in regular ESL programmes at the same grade level, as well as with learners who had received a comparable number of hours of instruction spread over a longer period of time. The results indicated that the intensive programme learners outperformed both comparison groups on tests of listening and reading comprehension and in oral fluency. In addition, although both regular and intensive programme learners were found to have very little contact with English prior to instruction, the intensive programme learners indicated somewhat greater contact after instruction. They also held more positive attitudes toward English than did the regular programme learners.

90–488 Vogel, Thomas (U. of Kiel, FRG) **and Bahns, Jens** (Pädagogische Hochschule Kiel, FRG). Introducing the English progressive in the classroom: insights from second language acquisition research. *System* (Oxford), **17,** 2 (1989), 183–93.

The main aim of this paper is to demonstrate the relevance of second language acquisition research to foreign language teaching. The area chosen for discussion is the English progressive aspect. German literature on foreign language teaching provides ample evidence that this area of English grammar constitutes a major problem for German students learning English. The background of the paper is a study by Vogel on the naturalistic acquisition of the English tense and aspect system by four German children. Some of his results are compared to the way in which – according to the textbooks – German teachers of English are supposed to introduce the English progressive in the classroom. Based on the results of this comparison, this paper makes some suggestions as to how the teaching of the progressive to beginners of English could be improved.

French

90–489 Bild, Eva-Rebecca and Swain, Merrill (Ontario Inst. for Studies in Ed., Toronto, Canada). Minority language students in a French immersion programme: their French proficiency. *Journal of Multilingual and Multicultural Development* (Clevedon, Avon), **10,** 3 (1989), 255–74.

Bilingual and unilingual students in a grade-eight English-French bilingual programme in Ontario were compared on measures of French proficiency. Forty-seven students were selected on the basis of their first language: English, Italian or a non-Romance language. French proficiency was measured using two written cloze tests and two oral story-telling tasks. One of each pair of tests was presented in a context-reduced condition and the other in a context-embedded condition. As hypothesised, bilinguals were found to perform significantly better than unilinguals on almost all the measures. No differences were discernible, however, with respect to their performance on context-embedded and context-reduced tasks. It was concluded that knowing a second language facilitates the learning of a third language and thus, bilingual children are excellent candidates for French immersion programmes.

Teaching particular languages

90–490 **Cicurel, Francine** and **Moirand, Sophie** (U. of Paris III, Crediscor). Apprendre à comprendre l'écrit: hypothèses didactiques. [Learning to understand writing: hypotheses for teaching.] *Français dans le Monde* (Paris), special no. Feb/Mar (1990), 147–57.

Approaches to understanding text have ranged from the 'bottom upwards' approach to the 'top downwards' approach, and have resulted in a 'mixed' model where there is constant reaction between the micro-text element such as word, morpheme, syllable etc., and the higher units of organisation such as sentence, phrase, clause and paragraph. The reader's performance is determined by his or her aim in reading, his or her prior cultural and linguistic knowledge and the characteristics of the text itself. The current global approach in French as a foreign language aims at an understanding of the text on several levels, not merely linear. This consists of scanning textual elements in order to form hypotheses about local and global meaning facilitating a recognition of the text type and strategic decisions about how it should be read – if at all. Teachers are trained in this by 'pre-pedagogic analysis' but methods differ according to French and Anglo-Saxon notions of discourse analysis. All centre round the addresser/addressee relations implied by the text and utilitarian matter tends to be chosen. Such texts tend to run in stereotypes against which the reader can more readily perceive the new and individual content.

However, a strategy based on the nature of texts will ignore or grate against individual approaches to reading and those induced by different cultures, particularly in reading French as a foreign language. Interpretation of graphic and layout conventions is an important element yet subject to wide cultural variation; and in what language does the foreign reader form his hypotheses, his own or that of the text?

90–491 **Edwards, Viviane** and **Rehorick, Sally**. Learning environments in immersion and non-immersion classrooms: are they different? *Canadian Modern Language Review* (Toronto), **46**, 3 (1990), 469–93.

This study examines one facet of French immersion education by comparing the learning environments of immersion and non-immersion classrooms in Grades 6, 7 and 9 in 95 New Brunswick classes. Environment is considered from the point of view of the students and how they perceive their relationship with their teachers, with their peers, with the subject studied and the methods used. At the Grade 6 level there are no significant differences in perception between immersion and non-immersion classes. At the Grade 7 level, students in immersion perceive their environment more positively than non-immersion students. By Grade 9, many of these differences have once again disappeared.

40–492 **Gremmo, Marie-José** and **Holec, Henri** (CRAPEL, U. of Nancy II). La compréhension orale: un processus et un comportement. [Oral comprehension: a process and a behaviour.] *Français dans le Monde* (Paris), special no. Feb/Mar (1990), 30–40.

Research on the psycholinguistics of listening is summarised, and its implications for the teaching of listening are explored. Listeners do not first identify the sounds which they have heard and then proceed from sound to meaning, but rather they form hypotheses about expected meaning and process the input in terms of their expectations, verifying or modifying as necessary. Even in our own language we do not always understand everything, but non-native listeners tend to be over-anxious about gaps in their understanding, and this is made worse by many teaching methods which aim at exhaustive comprehension and thus discourage learner initiative.

A range of activities should be provided with the specific purpose of fostering the sub-skills of listening. Some of these will actually be listening activities, but there will also be other kinds, of which some, e.g. giving information on the target culture, may even be done in the mother tongue. The approach should be cognitive, encouraging learner reflection, and authentic texts should be used as far as possible. In real life we listen for a purpose, either selectively, or for global meaning, or for details, or for background noise (radio, etc.), and pedagogic listening activities should likewise include a clearly specified reason for listening.

French

90–493 Grenet, Jean-Jack. Le français en Europe: combien de divisions? [French in Europe: how many divisions does it have?] *Français dans le Monde* (Paris), **230** (1990), 29–30.

Faced with the challenge of English, which is perceived as the easiest and most useful language of the European Community, French has to justify itself on other grounds, not the traditional one of being the language of a cultural élite taught by the most boring methods, but as the second major language of a pluralistic Europe and as the lingua franca of a large part of Africa. Such is the argument of a recent report by Martine Storti and the protagonists of French need to ask themselves the question 'What real strengths has French got?' As many EC school curricula now turn to English and push French into second place, there is no point in trying to recover a pre-eminence that is now lost but every reason to seek a new justification within the European context.

90–494 Heller, Monica. French immersion in Canada: a model for Switzerland? *Multilingua* (Amsterdam), **9**, 1 (1990), 67–85.

Canadian French immersion, a pedagogical programme involving French as a language of instruction for English-speaking children, has often been taken as a model for ways of improving intergroup relations. In this paper, a critical analysis of French immersion and French immersion research is presented, focusing on the impact of immersion on French–English relations. On the basis of this analysis, it is argued that it is necessary to examine second language instruction as a social, economic and political process embedded in relations of power. Before any specific model can be extended to new contexts, the local, particular manifestations of this process must be taken into account.

90–495 Nobili, Paola (U. of Bologna, Italy). La periphrase: une technique pour améliorer la compétence lexicale des adultes. [Paraphrase: a technique for improving the lexical competence of adult learners.] *Français dans le Monde* (Paris), special no. Feb/Mar (1990), 159–69.

Two groups of adults learning French in Italy (22 women in all aged between 47 and 68), were tested to discover what techniques, resources and strategies were available to them when asked to provide French equivalents of Italian words. In spite of differences between the two groups (Group A having a higher educational level than Group B), paraphrase proved to be the most fruitful method of eliciting French vocabulary for all the women, and one with considerable potential as a means of enabling learners to overcome lexical shortcomings and of assisting the weaker students to attain communicative competence.

90–496 Valdman, Albert. Sur la contribution de la linguistique structuraliste à l'enseignement du français aux États-Unis. [On the contribution of structural linguistics to the teaching of French in the United States.] *Etudes de Linguistique Appliquée* (Paris), **77** (1990), 7–19.

If acquiring an understanding of language structure and considering the links between language on the one hand and thought and society on the other hand, are taken to be central objectives of teaching languages in a formal setting with guided learning, then structural linguistics has an important contribution to make. This article compares traditional and structuralist descriptions of the forms of the adjective and the verb in French, and shows how structuralist descriptions have, for the first time, thrown light on the morphophonological structure of spoken French. On the other hand, as it is propped up by a reductionist psycholinguistic model and has taken no account of sociolinguistic factors, its illumination of the processes of learning and mastering a foreign language shows it to be insignificant. The article concludes by indicating some recent approaches in linguistics which promise to identify these processes and thus facilitate learning a foreign or second language.

Teaching particular languages

90–497 Wesche, M. B. and others. French immersion: postsecondary consequences for individuals and universities. *Canadian Modern Language Review* (Toronto), **46,** 3 (1990), 430–51.

The article reports the results of the first stage of an ongoing study of Ottawa area French immersion graduates. All of these students completed either early or late immersion programmes plus approximately one third of their secondary studies in French, and attended one of four universities in Eastern Ontario and Montreal. A detailed picture is given of the French language use skills of these students. The study also addresses their use of French in university studies, work and social life, and their attitudes toward its use. In addition, it describes opportunities for the use and retention of advanced French second language skills at the four institutions, and the methodology and instruments developed for the project which may be useful for similar studies elsewhere.

German

90–498 Brenez, Michelle (Lycée de Sèvres). Stratégies pour apprendre. [Learning strategies.] *Langues Modernes* (Paris), **84,** 1 (1990), 35–45.

Many techniques and strategies are described to assist French secondary pupils learning German at all ages and levels to consolidate and extend their knowledge of that language, to acquire good learning habits, to use their knowledge of German for their own purposes, and ultimately to assume responsibility for their own learning. Learner autonomy is not, however, to be achieved without advice and follow-up and much hard work on the part of the language teacher.

90–499 Cox, Susan and others (King's Coll. London). A tailor-made database for language teaching material. *Literary and Linguistic Computing* (Oxford), **4,** 4 (1989), 260–4.

A database for language teaching material has been developed in two research projects: one containing material for German as a second language at the Freie Universität Berlin, the other material for German for special purposes at King's College London.
This article describes the educational rationale of developing a database rather than working on new material and of designing a particularly user-friendly database rather than using available database software. In addition to this, it introduces readers to the use of the program by describing the *output option* and discusses the implications of such a database for the development of new material.

Spanish

90–500 Faltis, Christian (U. of Nevada, Reno). Spanish for native speakers: Freirian and Vygotskian perspectives. *Foreign Language Annals* (New York), **23,** 2 (1990), 117–26.

This article offers an alternative to the two approaches to teaching Spanish to adolescent and college level bilingual native speakers interested in developing their Spanish abilities. The argument is made that both the 'limited normative' and the 'comprehensive' approaches to Spanish for native speakers (SNS) strongly reflect synthetic and banking education curricular perspectives. Consequently, students are denied a voice in a curriculum that ignores social, historical and individual matters of concern. An alternative approach to SNS is identified and discussed. This approach draws heavily on Paulo Freire's problem-posing procedure for critical dialogue, and Lev Vygotsky's theory of social learning. The Freirian perspective gives primacy to critical reflection and action, with language development as a by-product of authentic purposeful social interaction among students and between the teacher and the students about topics that matter to students. The Vygotskian perspective shows why social interaction leads to individual learning and language development. Together, the two perspective offer a viable alternative to extant approaches to teaching Spanish to native bilingual speakers.

Spanish

90–501 Jensen, John B. (Florida International U.). On the mutual intelligibility of Spanish and Portuguese. *Hispania* (Worcester, Ma), **72,** 4 (1989), 848–52.

Though there is considerable mutual intelligibility as between Spanish and Portuguese, both on the visual and oral channels, it is debatable just what the overlap is and whether what holds good for the European languages also holds good for their Latin American counterparts. An experiment was conducted in San Paolo and Florida with native speakers of the respective languages being given listening comprehension material in the other language. The experiment is described and the results tabulated.

It was concluded that Spanish and Portuguese are 50–60% mutually intelligible by the oral/aural channel and that native speakers of Portuguese have a slight advantage. Brazilians did not show hostility to learning Spanish as had been anticipated. The results show that the ACTFL *Guidelines* in the proficiency testing of Spanish-speaking Portuguese students are inappropriate since completely untutored listeners can already score up to 50%.

90–502 Lodares Marrodan, Juan Ramón. Aplicaciones lexemáticas a la enseñanza del vocabulario. [Lexematic applications in the teaching of vocabulary.] *Revista de la AEPE* (Madrid, Spain), **36/7,** (1989), 33–44

Twenty years ago Coseriu proposed eight categories by which the lexicon could be structured into lexemes; as not all are useful for teaching purposes, five categories are proposed: (1) lexical field, (2) modification, (3) development, (4) composition, and (5) combinatory group. Lexical class, such as animate/inanimate or human/non-human is rejected as being debatable and of no pedagogic use. Examples of each category are quoted in tables, that of lexical field taking up most space as a variety of oppositions limiting each field is reviewed. The examples are mostly from Spanish though some are in English and the principle applies to any language.

The poverty of student vocabulary, whether in foreign language or mother tongue, is something which teachers have a duty to remedy; the structuring of the lexicon in this way can assist students in building up their vocabulary.

90–503 Terrell, Tracy David (U. of California, San Diego). Trends in the teaching of grammar in Spanish language textbooks. *Hispania* (Worcester, Ma), **73,** 1 (1990), 201–11.

With the focus on communication in language learning has come a re-evaluation of the role of grammar teaching. This paper introduces a framework for describing methodological trends in current beginning level Spanish texts for colleges and universities. The framework consists of five parameters: (a) communication activities/grammar exercises; (b) contextualisation/non-contextualisation; (c) meaningful/role; (d) open/closed (divergent/convergent); and (e) interactive/non-interactive. Examination of textbooks showed that they are qualitatively and quantitatively different from Spanish texts of the 'sixties and 'seventies. Methodological innovations as described in the five parameters had been incorporated into most of the textbooks.

Research in the supporting sciences

Phonetics and phonology

90–504 Fokes, Joann and Bond, Z. S. (Ohio U.). The vowels of stressed and unstressed syllables in non-native English. *Language Learning* (Ann Arbor, Mich), **39,** 3 (1989), 341–73.

Non-native and native American English speakers produced two-syllable words such as *confess* and *confirm* and three- and four-syllable derived words such as *confession* and *confirmation* in isolation and in sentences. The durations and formant patterns of the vowels were measured for the first two syllables of each word. In addition, the ratio of vowel-to-syllable was calculated for the syllable {con}. The non-native speakers had most difficulty with the four-syllable words, producing a vowel of variable quality in the first syllable and failing to reduce the vowel of the second syllable. In addition, the non-native speakers failed to produce appropriate durations for vowels according to position in word and stress pattern.

90–505 Ladefoged, Peter. Some reflections on the IPA. *UCLA Working Papers in Phonetics* (Los Angeles, Ca), **74** (1990), 61–76.

This paper is a commentary on both the newly revised International Phonetic Alphabet, and on the 1989 Kiel Convention of the International Phonetic Association at which it was produced. The new IPA chart is examined, and the pragmatic but conservative attitudes of the Association are described. It is shown that the IPA has a phonological basis, and that an IPA transcription has two parts: a text containing IPA symbols, and a set of conventions (rules) for interpreting the symbols. The paper concludes with a personal view of the problems of whether there is a finite set of speech sounds, and whether a sound in one language can be equated with one in another, suggesting that for the phonetician there is no universal truth independent of the observer.

Sociolinguistics

90–506 Andres, Franz. Language relations in multilingual Switzerland. *Multilingua* (Amsterdam), **9,** 1 (1990), 11–45.

The purpose of this paper is to provide a framework for the discussion of the project 'Unterrichtssprache Französich/Deutsch (UFD)'. Part I summarises the most pertinent political, socio-economic and historical aspects of Switzerland as a nation, as far as these aspects are relevant for the objectives of the project. Part II contains an account of the status of the four language groups and the relationship between them. In this part space is given to discussing the status and prospects of Italian and Romansch as national languages, although they are not included in the scope of the project as yet. [See also 90–515.]

90–507 Görlach, Manfred. Word-formation and the ENL-ESL-EFL distinction. *English World-wide* (Heidelberg, FRG), **10,** 2 (1989), 279–313.

A comparative study of English word-formation aims to determine whether we can correlate distinctions in the status of English in various speech communities with a set of distinctive features which would make it possible to identify the source of specific texts. Newspapers and dictionaries are used as source material for the study of English in six contemporary settings: in Scotland (ESD), in 'colonial' contexts such as the USA and Australia, in bi- and multilingual communities, in Creole-speaking communities and in second and foreign language situations [discussion with examples]. It is difficult to systematise the field of word-formation sufficiently to provide a statistically significant typology; more data are necessary and phonology and syntax may prove more rewarding areas of investigation. While ENL-ESL-EFL are useful terms to express differences in the status of English in societies, differences are less important on the level of systems and norms, being more concerned with individual competence.

Sociolinguistics

90–508 **MacKinnon, Kenneth and Densham, Jenny** (Hatfield Poly., Watford, Herts). Ethnolinguistic diversity in Britain: policies and practice in school and society. *Language, Culture and Curriculum* (Clevedon, Avon), **2**, 2 (1989), 75–89.

The paper describes the efforts of three indigenous minority-language communities in Britain (Scottish Gaelic, Welsh, and British Sign Language) to achieve mother-tongue education. It argues that their experiences illustrate aspects of social structure in Britain that are overlooked in conventional class analysis. The reluctance of the UK in the past to cater for the linguistic and cultural needs of the indigenous minorities is linked to present difficulties in coping with the immigrant minorities and with the demand for EC languages in preparation for the Internal European Market of 1992. Assimilationist assumptions still underlie current policies and practice. Multilingualism is seen as a transitional phenomenon, and acculturation as the exchange of one culture for another rather than the acquisition of bicultural or bilingual identities and abilities. Ethnic diversity is presented as a problem, not as societal enrichment. The paper draws parallels between the teaching of the indigenous languages and the teaching of ethnic and EC languages. A synthesis is proposed in the form of a multilingual educational programme based on the UNESCO resolution of 1951 on the universal right to mother-tongue education.

90–509 **Man-Siu Yau** (Chinese U. of Hong Kong). The controversy over teaching medium in Hong Kong – an analysis of a language policy. *Journal of Multilingual and Multicultural Development* (Clevedon, Avon), **10**, 4 (1989), 279–95.

This paper analyses a language plan proposed by the Hong Kong government to promote Chinese-medium education. A brief history of the past language situation in the secondary school system is first provided followed by an outline of the evolution of the proposed plan. Then the targets set up in the plan are examined against the background of the existing language requirements in the field of education and employment. Since the English-biased linguistic infrastructure in the wider social setting does not correlate with the targets to be promoted in school, it is predicted that the proposed plan will not achieve much success. Moreover, the failure of the plan may even lead to the perpetuation of the inferiority of Chinese-medium education.

90–510 **Mar-Molinero, Clare** (U. of Southampton). The teaching of Catalan in Catalonia. *Journal of Multilingual and Multicultural Development* (Clevedon, Avon), **10**, 4 (1989), 307–26.

One of the greatest challenges the language planners in Catalonia face in their drive to promote Catalan to an equal status with Castilian is that of teaching the language to the large non-Catalan population now found in Catalonia. This paper examines the provision of Catalan and the use of Catalan as a medium in Catalonia's education system at all levels. A new legal framework has allowed the local Catalan government considerable scope to upgrade the teaching of Catalan. Whether resources and the support from the community are sufficient, and whether the policy favours Catalan aggressively enough to prevent Castilian remaining always the dominant partner are discussed.

90–511 **Mulac, Anthony** (U. of Santa Barbara, Ca). Men's and women's talk in same-gender and mixed-gender dyads: power or polemic? *Journal of Language and Social Psychology* (Clevedon, Avon), **8**, 3/4 (1989), 249–70.

One hundred and eight university students (54 men and 54 women) were recorded in 108, eight-minute, problem-solving interactions under two dyadic conditions: (*a*) same-gender, and (*b*) mixed-gender. Interactants were coded during each minute for: (*a*) amount of Talk, (*b*) Mean Length Utterance (MLU) and (*c*) Rate. MANOVA results for Talk indicated that men in mixed-gender dyads talked more than did men and women in same-gender dyads, and they in turn talked more than women in mixed-gender dyads. For MLU, men consistently spoke in longer utterances, regardless of gender of their partner. No Rate differences were found involving gender. Additionally, when there was a control for interactant gender, individuals who talked more and in longer utterances were rated by their partners as higher in Dynamism, an operationalisation of power. Finally, multiple regression analyses indicated that the Talk and MLU differences found were more predictable on the basis of gender than Androgyny, Empathy or Social Desirability. The findings suggest that gender leads to differences in talk behaviour that are consistent with the appearance, but not necessarily the actual implementation, of power.

90–512 Nehr, Monika. The acquisition of literacy in bilingual education: Turkish schoolchildren in West Germany. *Multilingua* (Amsterdam), **9,** 1 (1990), 87–103.

The present article discusses the various social, psychological and educational problems associated with bilingual literacy teaching. The discussion centres in particular on problems experienced by Turkish schoolchildren in West German schools. It advocates a simultaneous and co-ordinated approach to bilingual literacy education. The article stresses the positive implications of the transfer process from mother tongue to second language as far as the acquisition of literacy is concerned. Throughout the article, emphasis is put on the fact that the methodology should be adapted to the children's communicative needs and sensibilities, taking their intercultural background into account.

90–513 Nelde, Peter Hans. Le plurilinguisme dans l'Europe multilingue – avec un regard sur 1993. [Plurilingualism in a multilingual Europe – with an eye on 1993.] *Multilingua* (Amsterdam), **9,** 1 (1990), 47–65.

A concept of conflict is first discussed, and then applied to several European multilingual situations. Conflict-laden causes for linguistic discord are illustrated by examples of officially multilingual countries, the minority problem and urban multilingualism.

What attempts have been made to avoid or overcome the resulting conflicts are shown by a series of plans which have been used in multilingual countries like Belgium. Since Europe, with its language conflicts often dating from the nineteenth century, has obviously not prepared sufficiently for a multilingual (partial) European Community in the year 1993, a few propositions for the acquisition of several languages should fan anew the discussion of a purposeful multilingualism that corresponds to the market. The article ends with a polemic look at the future of multilingual Europe.

90–514 Rampton, Ben (U. of Southampton). Some unofficial perspectives on bilingualism and education for all. *Language Issues* (Birmingham), **3,** 2 (1990), 27–32.

The recommendations of the Swann report on the education of children from ethnic minorities are challenged in the light of research into informal language behaviour within mixed-race friendship groups. Swann's assumption that relations among the youth are strained, and that only school can improve them, is refuted by a study of the recreational use of Panjabi by white and Afro-Caribbean adolescents. The phenomenon of joking abuse and the spread of *bhangra*, originally Panjabi folk music, in new forms, are connected with group allegiances and testify to close mixed friendships. In this context, it is suggested that language awareness programmes in schools would be valuable in responding to the developing sense of a multilingual community. Whereas the Swann report opposes bilingual teaching, fearing social division, the evidence from this study suggests that separate language provision for youngsters of Indian and Pakistani descent does not undermine the sense of loyalty that their friends feel towards them, but rather reinforces admiration for the ethnically specific knowledge to be gained. Indeed, the possibility of providing bilingual education for majority monolinguals must not be dismissed. Emphasis is laid on the importance of attending to the sociolinguistic dynamics of youth culture when making educational policy decisions.

90–515 Stotz, Daniel and Andres, Franz. Problems in developing bilingual education programmes in Switzerland. *Multilingua* (Amsterdam), **9,** 1 (1990), 113–36.

On the basis of the preceding contributions to this issue, this paper presents the project 'Unterrichtssprache Französisch/Deutsch' (UFD), which was undertaken by an interdisciplinary group of re-

90–516 Tay, Mary W. J. (National U. of Singapore). Code switching and code mixing as a communicative strategy in multilingual discourse. *World Englishes* (Oxford), **8**, 3 (1989), 407–17.

While the formal characteristics of code switching and mixing, such as free morpheme constraints and equivalence constraints, have been well documented across a variety of languages, relatively little is known about how code switching and mixing are used as communicative strategies in a multilingual community. This paper is an attempt to fill this gap. It examines various spoken texts which involve code switching and mixing between some of the main languages spoken in Singapore, such as English, Mandarin, Hokkien and Teochew. The analysis demonstrates how code switching and mixing are used as a communicative strategy, as a device for elucidation and interpretation, to establish solidarity and rapport in multilingual discourse. Despite differences in the formal characteristics of the languages concerned, common communicative strategies have evolved as a result of languages in contact. This paper also discusses the linguistic, psychological and sociolinguistic implications of studies on code mixing and switching. It argues that such studies help us to better understand the function and forms of language used in a dynamic, multilingual community. This paper concludes with a plea to look at languages in multilingual communities as independent systems instead of as merely deviant or different forms of native English.

Psycholinguistics

90–517 Boland, Julie E. and others (U. of Rochester). Lexical projection and the interaction of syntax and semantics in parsing. *Journal of Psycholinguistic Research* (New York), **18**, 6 (1989), 563–76.

A series of self-paced reading studies utilised an embedded anomaly technique to investigate long-distance dependencies with dative verbs. Previous research in the lab demonstrated that argument structure influences the gap-filling process. Experiment 1 extended that work by demonstrating that dative verbs pattern with other complex transitive verbs (i.e., a fronted filler that is implausible as the direct object will not be interpreted as the direct object until the absence of a noun phrase after the verb forces the postulation of a direct object gap. This pattern contrasts with that of transitive verbs that subcategorise for a single internal argument position, where fronted fillers are obligatorily interpreted as the direct object). Experiments 2 and 3 investigate the prediction that semantic analyses precede syntactic analyses in dative questions. It is argued that the lexical information about argument structure and thematic roles can guide semantic interpretation.

90–518 Charles-Luce, Jan and Luce, Paul A. (State U. of New York at Buffalo). Similarity neighbourhoods of words in young children's lexicons. *Journal of Child Language* (Cambridge), **17**, 1 (1990), 205–15.

Similarity neighbourhoods for words in young children's lexicons were investigated using three computerised databases. These databases were representative of three groups of native English speakers: 5-year-olds, 7-year-olds, and adults. Computations relating to the similarity neighbourhoods of words in the children's and adult's lexicon revealed that words in the 5- and 7-year-old's lexicons have many fewer similar neighbours than the same words analysed in the adult lexicon. Thus, young children may employ more global recognition strategies because words are more discriminable in memory. The neighbourhood analyses provide a number of insights into the processes of auditory word recognition in children and the possible structural organisation of words in the young child's mental lexicon.

90–519 Greene, John O. (Purdue U., West Lafayette, Ind). *Journal of Language and Social Psychology* (Clevedon, Avon), **8**, 3/4 (1989), 193–220.

Two decades of extensive research and intense debate have served to make clear that human behaviour is characterised by both stability and variation over time and across situations. It remains, however, to articulate a coherent theoretical account detailing the processes of person–situation interaction that give rise to this consistency and discriminativeness. Toward this end, requirements for an adequate interactional theory are reviewed. Central to the approach taken here is the assumption that because consistency and discriminativeness are properties of behaviour, these phenomena are likely to be understood only by recourse to models of behavioural production. The second section of the article then summarises a cognitive model specifying the structures and control processes comprising the behavioural output system. This model permits a reconceptualisation of individual dispositions and situational influences in terms consistent with the properties of the output system. Finally, the model is extended to the realm of nonverbal behaviour to make explicit claims concerning those conditions under which behavioural stability should be enhanced.

90–520 Haberlandt, Karl (Trinity Coll.) **and Graesser, Arthur C.** (Memphis State U.). Buffering new information during reading. *Discourse Processes* (Norwood, NJ), **12**, 4 (1989), 479–94.

Results are reported from two subject-paced reading experiments in which word-reading times were collected using the moving-window method. Word type, the amount of information at successive locations within sentences, and task were the independent variables, and word-reading time was the dependent variable. Reading times increased with successive locations, as indexed by the cumulative number of new arguments per sentence. There was an interaction involving word type, such that reading times of content words increased more steeply than reading times of function words. Among content words, the increase was steeper for nouns than for verbs; and, among nouns, the increase was steeper for new nouns than for repeated nouns. The results are discussed in terms of buffer models of reading, the processing of different lexical classes, and hypotheses which predict serial position effects.

90–521 Hadar, Uri (Charing Cross and Westminster Medical School, London). Two types of gesture and their role in speech production. *Journal of Language and Social Psychology* (Clevedon, Avon), **8**, 3/4 (1989), 221–8.

Speech is normally accompanied by numerous body movements such as hand gestures, head nods, posture changes, etc. These are known to have communicative and regulatory functions such as clarifying or emphasising messages, regulating speaking turns, etc. In addition and in parallel to these, it is argued, body movements have specific speech productive functions, primarily the facilitation of lexical selection and the regulation of prosodic features. Movements serving the two functions differ in many ways, e.g. in their kinematic properties, complexity, timing in relation to speech, impairment in aphasia, mode of encoding and the stages of speech processing in which they originate. These differences are emergent, rather than prescriptive or rule-governed, originating in cognitive and motor constraints. The functional utilisation of body movement is locally optional.

90–522 Hoff-Ginsberg, Erika (U. of Wisconsin-Parkside). Maternal speech and the child's development of syntax: a further look. *Journal of Child Language* (Cambridge), **17**, 1 (1990), 85–99.

This study compared four categories of maternal utterances that were found in a previous study to predict children's rates of syntax development to a category of maternal utterances that was unrelated to syntax development. The comparisons were designed to test the hypotheses that maternal utterances which benefit syntax development do so by providing syntactically rich data or by eliciting conversation from the child. Data-providing and conversation-eliciting characteristics of the selected categories of maternal utterances were assessed from the same transcripts of 22 mothers interacting with their $2\frac{1}{2}$-year-old children that had provided the database for the earlier study of predictive relations. Each of the three positive predictor categories of maternal utterances differed from the unrelated category – in more frequently illustrating the affected aspect of syntax development, in eliciting more speech from the child, or both. Neither of these characteristics was true of the negative predictor category. The pattern of results suggested that maternal speech supports the child's development of syntax by engaging the child in linguistic interaction and also by providing illustrations of the structures the child acquires.

90–523 **Osterhout, Lee** (Northwestern U., Ill) **and Swinney, David A.** (CUNY). On the role of the simplicity heuristic in language processing: evidence from structural and inferential processing. *Journal of Psycholinguistic Research* (New York), **18,** 6 (1989), 553–62.

This paper evaluates whether or not simplicity or 'minimalistic' heuristics, which are posited to account for local ambiguity resolution at the level of structural processing and for the lack of inferential elaboration during discourse processing, represent the most accurate account of language processing. Evidence from on-line studies is presented which suggests that alternative, more knowledge-based mechanisms for handling processing are brought to bear in these situations.

90–524 **Tomasello, Michael** (Emory U.) **and others.** Young children's conversations with their mothers and fathers: differences in breakdown and repair. *Journal of Child Language* (Cambridge), **17,** 1 (1990), 115–30.

This study compared the conversations of mothers and fathers with their children at 1;3 and 1;9, with special attention to breakdown-repair sequences. It was found that, overall, children and secondary caregiver fathers experienced more communicative breakdowns than did children and primary caregiver mothers. More specifically, fathers requested clarification of their children more often than did mothers, and they most often used a non-specific query (e.g. *What?*). Mothers used more specific queries (e.g. *Put it where?*) and were involved in more 'looped' sequences involving multiple requests for clarification. Fathers also failed to acknowledge child utterances more often than did mothers. After a father non-acknowledgement, children tended not to persist and when they did they often received further non-acknowledgements; the dyad did not often return to the child's original topic. After a maternal non-acknowledgement, on the other hand, children persisted and the dyad more often returned to its previous topic. The results are interpreted as support for the Bridge Hypothesis which claims that fathers present children with communicative challenges that help prepare them for communication with less familiar adults.

90–525 **Walker, Michael B. and Trimboli, Antonietta** (U. of Sydney, N.S.W., Australia). Communicating affect: the role of verbal and nonverbal content. *Journal of Language and Social Psychology* (Clevedon, Avon), **8,** 3/4 (1989), 229–48.

The role of nonverbal signals in communicating affect is not well understood. Recent research has both emphasised and played down the importance of the nonverbal signals relative to what is said. A careful examination of the evidence shows that the data in favour of and against nonverbal dominance come from two different empirical approaches. It is argued that both approaches are methodologically unsound. A new approach to the question is developed based on the assumption that the communication channel which maintains the affective tone of the interaction is the primary channel by which affect is being communicated. The affective tone of the interaction can be established by examining the communicational context for any given message. This assumption allows mixed messages, in which the verbal and nonverbal channels are conveying opposed affective tones, to be analysed for channel dominance. Sixteen segments from interviews televised live were examined. In twelve of the sixteen segments the nonverbal channels carried the affective tone. A detailed

Pragmatics

90–526 **Longacre, Robert E.** (U. of Texas at Arlington). Two hypotheses regarding text generation and analysis. *Discourse Processes* (Norwood, NJ), **12,** 4 (1989), 413–60.

It is proposed here that in any language and for any discourse type within that language the verb forms/clause structures can be arranged in a rank scheme in which a mainline of discourse development is encoded by a characteristic construction (or a very limited set of constructions) while lines of subsidiary development, which represent progressive degrees of departure from the mainline, are encoded in other constructions. It is further proposed that this graded salience scheme can then provide guidelines for the analysis of local spans of text (paragraphs) so that sentences whose independent clauses have constructions which are high in the salience schemes are dominant over ancillary sentences which have constructions which are lower in the scheme. The first hypothesis has more to do with text generation, while the second has to do with text analysis. The two hypotheses are meant to yield salience schemes and constituent analyses which mutually corroborate and correct each other. These hypotheses and their reciprocity are illustrated here relative to narrative discourse in eight languages in five distinct linguistic areas.

90–527 **Wildner-Basset, Mary E.** (U. of Arizona). The clanger phenomenon and the foreign language learner. *IRAL* (Heidelberg, FRG), **28,** 1 (1990), 27–42.

Conversation between a native speaker and a language learner usually involves an asymmetrical power relationship, with the latter at a disadvantage. It is proposed that an understanding of the 'clanger' phenomenon may enable the learner to participate in a negotiation of identity and thereby contribute to the reduction of this disadvantage. The 'clanger' is defined as an aggressive utterance which has a disruptive effect on conversation; its purpose is to redefine the relationship between the participants. An example is utterance B(2) in the following extract:
A(1): Sir, I would like to explain to you how terribly senseless and immoral it is to be poisoning our environment with...
B(1): What did you say?
A(2): Sir, I would like to expl...
B(2): Aw shuddup, freak!

Since 'clangers' are interpreted as showing an increase in dominance or hostility, their misuse has potentially serious interactional consequences. It is crucial for the teacher to distinguish between their intentional and appropriate use and accidental and deviant usage, which is manifested not only in verbal and prosodic features but also in concomitant facial expressions and gestures.

Language description and use

Descriptive studies of particular languages

English

90–528 Cheshire, Jenny and others. Urban British dialect grammar: the question of dialect levelling. *English World-wide* (Heidelberg, FRG). **10,** 2 (1989), 185–225.

The Survey of British Dialect Grammar was carried out between 1986 and 1989. Its main aims were to increase our knowledge of the morphology and syntax of BrE dialects, and to consider the educational implications arising from the coexistence of Standard English and dialect grammar. The Survey responses indicated those features that are most widespread in urban varieties of BrE, including some not usually included, such as *should of*. Some features widely reported are thought to be used by 'educated' speakers so should perhaps not be considered as nonstandard, such as *there's* and *there was*, *never* as past tense negator, and (possibly) adverbial *quick*. All these features are characteristic of spoken English, and children have to learn not to use them in their school writing. Perhaps such features should be thought of as 'social dialect' features rather than as regional dialect features, but their social distribution has not yet been determined.

Spanish

90–529 Miles, Cecil. About the Spanish verb 'haber'. *Canadian Modern Language Review* (Toronto), **46,** 2 (1990), 317–23.

A number of aspects of the Spanish verb *haber* present conundrums as to their meanings and derivations which are far from being resolved. Apart from its familiar (and recent) function as an auxiliary in the so-called 'perfect' tenses, its underlying meaning 'to have, to hold' still persists in the impersonal *hay* (a close relative of *il y a*) while other morphemes previously associated with *haber* may prove to be quite unrelated.

Translation

90–530 Dubois, Betty Lou. Thematisation across machine and human translation: English to French. *IRAL* (Heidelberg, FRG), **28,** 1 (1990), 43–65.

To investigate the effects of translation on thematisation, primary level (main clause) themes from the 463 independent clauses of an English journal article of high level physics popularisation were categorised according to status, unmarked, marked, or rhematised, using the analytic framework of Dubois and, as appropriate, syntactic form. Their distribution across three major sentence types in the 13 sections of the article was computed. Clauses of the article were compared first to a selection of those of an unpublished French machine translation and then to those of a published human translation, with thematic changes reported in detail for the latter. The automatic translation is generally faithful to the original thematisation, but confronted with the complexities of the English noun phrase or with the gaps in its own lexicon, the machine can lose or create a theme or even garble one. As might be expected, machine errors are repetitive. The themes of the human translation, on the other hand, are perfectly comprehensible, but substantially transformed. There are 14 cases of combinations of English independent clauses, 17 of splitting of complex clauses, all of which alter primary thematisation. In the remaining clauses, there are extensive changes in thematisation, the most important being thematisation to a pronoun or to existential *il y a*. It is suggested that fidelity to thematisation is one criterion by which to judge the quality of a translation.

Language description and use

90–531 Hartmann, R. R. K. (Exeter U.). The not so harmless drudgery of finding translation equivalents. *Language and Communication* (Oxford), **10**, 1 (1990), 47–55.

Compiling a bilingual dictionary is a complex task involving an attempt to find equivalents in pairs of languages. Both linguistic and non-linguistic factors are probably included. It is agreed today that the best translations are those which make use of adaptation strategies and interpretation of the original text, and focus on the target language taking into account social and psychological factors, and the purpose of the text. It is recognised that there are equivalence types ranging from non-existent through partial to complete. Equivalents are easier to establish in pairs of languages of similar ancestry, such as European languages, but in a Chinese–English dictionary for example, the many linguistic and cultural differences make the task more difficult and require a process of gradual and complicated development from literal translation through to full equivalence.

A bilingual dictionary should offer lexical equivalents in the target language rather than explanatory paraphrases or definitions, and such equivalents can be established through analysis of parallel texts. However, parallel texts provide equivalence only in terms of a particular use of a word in a certain context. Variables of use and context, and other meanings of a word render equivalence only partial or approximate. Comparison of initial entries for 'F' in a study of two recently published monolingual dictionaries, German and English, and the *Collins German–English dictionary*, revealed various shortcomings such as omission of the possibility of zero equivalence, translation loss, and circumlocution.

Analysis of parallel texts, although not explaining how equivalents are arrived at, could assist research into ways of establishing equivalents, and computers could be used to generate equivalents by scanning parallel texts and to store information concerning the matching operation. There is at present little conclusive information which could help teachers in the training of translators and lexicographers.

90–532 Wilss, Wolfram. Cognitive aspects of the translation process. *Language and Communication* (Oxford), **10**, 1 (1990), 19–36.

The current objective of translation science is to provide a framework to explain the cognitive processes involved in the activity of translation. A theory of translation must have an empirical foundation and provide a practical and efficient framework for the activity. Examples of cognitive processes are analysis, interpretation, comparison, and the weighing of possibilities, all of which are required to harmonise two different linguistic and cultural entities.

By its nature, translation is a complex activity in which the translator is the intermediary between the writer of the source text and the reader of the target text. Although certain specialised text types, such as technical or commercial texts, are not too difficult to translate because of a degree of similarity in source and target languages, other types may cause severe problems because of semantic vagueness, syntactic complexity, metaphors, etc. Consequently, in order to create a text appropriate for its purpose, the translator requires to revise the work at various stages, to use imagination and inventiveness, and to apply competent decision-making strategies. However, caution must be exercised in the uncertain areas of creativity and intuition.

New books

Short annotations of recent publications, which aim to be informative and objective but not critical, together with a list of books received. Textbooks are only occasionally annotated.

Barbour, Stephen and Stevenson, Patrick
Variation in German: a critical approach to German sociolinguistics. Cambridge University Press, 1990. xiii + 308 pp. £35.00 (£11.95 pb).

This book examines the interrelations between language and society in the German-speaking countries. The questions 'What is German and who speaks it?' and 'How does the language vary dependent on social, political and geographical factors?' are addressed and placed in their historical context. This is a comprehensive account of major topics in the contemporary study of German sociolinguistics, and includes the history and development of the German language, German as a minority language, minority languages in German-speaking countries, traditional dialects, variation in contemporary colloquial speech, the influence of English on German, and German in East and West. It draws together much otherwise inaccessible material from a great range of sources. The authors also assess critically research work carried out in German-speaking countries: this is the first book on this area to be written from a standpoint outside the German-speaking tradition of linguistic studies, and the most detailed account yet to appear in English of German sociolinguistics. This book extends and complements Michael Clyne's *Language and society in the German-speaking countries.*

Britton, James and others (eds.)
Teaching and learning English worldwide. Clevedon, Avon: Multilingual Matters, 1990. 338 pp. £48.00 (£16.95 pb).

This book contains historical studies of the teaching of English in different countries where English is a mother tongue language or a significant second, or in some cases, third language. The authors of the various chapters have concentrated on the place of English in a particular society and have attempted to describe how the teaching of English exists in the social and political context of that society and how it is shaped as a school subject and/or language of instruction in that context. The authors are all familiar with the recent history of English teaching in their respective countries, and, in all cases, have themselves been significant contributors to that history. This being so, they write with a strongly held point of view about the significance of English as a school subject and its place in the social milieu.

This volume was produced under the aegis of the International Federation for the Teaching of English.

Clark, John and Yallop, Colin
An introduction to phonetics and phonology. Oxford: Blackwell, 1990. xiv + 400 pp. £40.00 (£14.95 pb).

Assuming no prior knowledge of the subject, this book offers a thorough account of topics covered in courses in phonetics and phonology. It is unusually comprehensive, including detailed attention to the fundamentals of speech production as well as to phonological description and analysis. The early chapters describe the organs of speech, survey the wide variety of speech sounds that can be found in the world's languages, and explain basic principles of phonological organisation. A separate chapter is devoted to the generative approach to phonology, and another to the acoustics of speech production, providing information that will prove valuable reference material. The phenomena of stress, tone and intonation are dealt with in a chapter on prosody, and several descriptive systems of speech components or features are also summarised and reviewed. The final chapter draws the book together by looking back over the theoretical issues that have been raised and by giving a historical survey of ways of thinking and talking about speech.

Duda, Richard and Riley, Philip (eds.)
Learning styles. Nancy, France: Presses Universitaires de Nancy, 1990. 234 pp. £21.50.

The concept of learning styles is attracting considerable attention among teachers and researchers. The recognition that variability in skills and approaches is characteristic of any group of learners is fostering a reappraisal of many current generalisations about language learning, be they tradition, communicative, or humanistic. The papers in this volume are a contribution to theory, experimentation and practice in the field of learning styles. Topics such as cognitive style, self-evaluation, learning conversations, communication strategies, experiential learning, autonomisation, language awareness and intercultural variation are discussed by 16 contributors from nine different European countries.

New books

Duff, Alan and Maley, Alan
Literature. Oxford: Oxford University Press, 1990 (Resource Books for Teachers series). 167 pp. £7.50.

This is an innovatory resource book which offers the teacher a wide variety of interesting and practical ideas for using literature in the language class. It is designed with the needs of the language learner in mind. No previous knowledge of literature is required either by the teacher or the students. It is not a book on how to study literature, but on how to use it for language practice.

Gołębiowska, Aleksandra
Getting students to talk. Hemel Hempstead, Herts: Prentice Hall, 1990 (revised edn. of *Let's talk*, 1987). xii + 161 pp. £6.55.

This book lays a sound foundation for fluent communicative discussion among students, gives ready made recipes for stimulating role-plays and isolates the language that students need to emulate in order to talk together effectively. Section 1: a thorough rationale to prepare teachers to initiate interaction with their classes. Section 2: ready-to-use simulations, discussions and role-plays on a variety of motivating topics. Section 3: a complete breakdown of functional language needed for the role-plays (particularly useful for non-native teachers).

Grimshaw, Allen D. (ed.)
Conflict talk: sociolinguistic investigations of arguments in conversations. Cambridge: Cambridge University Press. x + 356 pp. £37.50 (£12.95 pb).

The 11 studies in this volume consider conflict talk, using analytic and interpretative perspectives to examine the disputes of adults and of children. Most of the studies are based on audio or sound-image records of naturally occurring discourse arising in a variety of contexts. These range from street to school, from courtroom to hospital, and from home to workplace. There is a short introductory chapter and extensive theoretical conclusion to the studies, which come from a variety of disciplines: the authors comprise anthropologists, linguists, sociologists, a lawyer and a psychologist.

Kenning, M-M. and Kenning, M. J.
Computers and language learning: current theory and practice. London: Ellis Horwood, 1990. 153 pp. £18.75.

This book attempts to step outside current software-dependent approaches and to set CALL in the wider context of contemporary trends and practices in language learning, the emphasis being theoretical rather than practical. Some fundamental issues in language learning and teaching are addressed with a view to finding out what lessons these hold for CALL. Chapter 1 discusses how the use of computers, which emphasise the written language, can be justified in the context of today's trend towards the development of oral proficiency. Chapter 2 considers current approaches to teaching content and syllabus design, while chapter 3 examines developments in teaching methodology and how the computer can be used. Chapter 4 looks at prevailing theories of language learning and the implications for the use of computer technology. Chapter 5 surveys affective factors which have a major influence on the learner's rate of progress, together with implications for CALL. Chapter 6 considers the computer's potential contribution to 'conscious' learning.

King, Ann
Degrees of fluency: a sixth-former's guide to language degree courses. London: CILT, 1990. 232 pp. £10.95.

This book offers practical advice to young people on how to extend their study of languages and equip themselves with marketable linguistic skills. A useful guide to the wide range of degree courses on offer.

Padilla, Amado M. and others (eds.)
Foreign language education: issues and strategies. London: Sage Publications, 1990. 256 pp. £29.95 (£14.95 pb).

The United States is currently facing a critical shortage of language-competent residents in a world where bilingualism and multilingualism are the norm. The changing American demography, along with an increasingly competitive international trade arena, suggest the need for a change in educational policy. The editors and contributors to this comprehensive volume share a professional commitment to assist in the development of a language-competent American society. Accordingly, they evaluate the historical, political and research perspectives of second-language instructional programmes in the first half of the book. The latter half is devoted to an evaluation of immersion education, including its design, implementation and evaluation. In particular, the authors discuss bilingual information processing and cognitive learning strategies, in addition to describing actual immersion programmes. The last section takes up content-based instruction and calls for continued innovation in language education.
[Companion volume to *Bilingual education: issues and strategies*: see below.]

New books

Padilla, Amado M. and others (eds.)

Bilingual education: issues and strategies. London: Sage Publications, 1990. 261 pp. £29.95 (£14.95 pb).

According to demographic projections, there will be more bilingual than monolingual children in the United States by the next century. Consequently the traditional emphasis on 'English-only' education, which seeks the homogenisation of linguistically diverse groups, will need to be re-evaluated in the face of the changing makeup of American society.

In this volume, the contributors advocate innovative instructional programmes designed to encourage the development of second-language skills for as broad a spectrum of school-age students as possible. To this end, they present the history, theory, and methods for developing effective bilingual education as well as the context for evaluating research findings and for the development of new pedagogical models. Part I provides an overview of the history of bilingual education as well as the context for evaluating research findings and for the development of new pedagogical models. Part II covers various issues in bilingual education, such as the relationship between language and thinking, and the role of children's native language in their early education. Part III explores curriculum development for classrooms, schools and districts as well as implementation and evaluation strategies. Part IV discusses how to apply the research and theory into practice in various disciplines, settings (grammar to college level), and in immersion programmes.
[Companion volume to *Foreign language education: issues and strategies*: see above.]

Pankhurst, James and others (eds.)

Learnability and second languages: a book of readings. Dordrecht: Foris, 1988. 207 pp. £29.05.

This book offers insights into the factors that constrain and promote the acquisition of second languages. It draws on research in theoretical linguistics which bears on the logical problem of how children come to know a language, the grammar of their mother tongue, with so little evidence. It deals with the relevance of such issues in adult, non-native grammatical acquisition and how such research might be conducted. In particular, the question of how other language knowledge may affect the manner and rate of development is considered, as also what the nature of evidence in a second language context is, and the role of universal grammar.

Richards, Brian J.

Language development and individual differences: a study of auxiliary verb learning. Cambridge: Cambridge University Press, 1990. xviii+252 pp. £32.50.

This study examines the variation between children in their early language development, focusing on their acquisition of the auxiliary verb. Learning auxiliary verbs and the syntactic and pragmatic functions with which they are associated is an essential component in the child's language development from an early stage. At the same time, children vary extensively in the age and stage at which auxiliaries emerge and also in the style and rate at which subsequent development takes place. Some aspects of this variation have been linked with the quality of interaction with the child's conversation partners, others with a tendency to acquire language holistically through unanalysed 'chunks'.

Using data drawn both from the Bristol Longitudinal Study of Language Development and from independent case studies conducted in Wales, Dr Richards points to a number of important areas of variation between children – for example in the sequence of syntax development and in the relationship between pragmatic and syntactic factors – and raises a number of important methodological and theoretical issues, such as how to assess the level of unanalysed usage and how to measure real syntactic advance. By analysing the relationship between input and rate of auxiliary growth, the study also attempts to resolve some of the inconsistencies in the results of previous input studies which have included the auxiliary as a measure.

Rost, Michael

Listening in language learning. Harlow, Middx: Longman, 1990 (Applied Linguistics and Language Study series). xviii+278 pp. £10.95.

This book provides a theoretical and practical discussion of the role of listening in language use and language learning. Although much work has been done on the development of oral communication skills in language education, the nature of listening problems in language use, the ways in which a learner's background influences understanding, and the means by which one's ability to listen can be improved have largely gone unexamined. The book provides a clear and authoritative guide to these issues, emphasising the importance of a combined cognitive, social and educational perspective in defining what listening ability is and explaining how listening may be used in improving language learning skills.

After the initial chapters have introduced listening from a cognitive perspective, the book provides a

New books

detailed investigation of listening in social and educational contexts, and concludes with an analysis of how listening development can be incorporated effectively into curriculum design. Discussion questions and exercises throughout the book allow the reader to investigate practically the role of listening in verbal interaction and language learning.

Rubagumya, C. M. (ed.)

Language in education in Africa. Clevedon, Avon: Multilingual Matters, 1990. 160 pp. £35.00 (£11.95 pb).

As early as 1953, UNESCO recommended the use of mother tongue in education. However, in most African countries today foreign (European) languages are still used as the media of instruction, especially at secondary and tertiary levels of education. The debate as to the advantages and disadvantages of using African languages in education goes on unabated. This book is a contribution to this debate.

Focusing on Tanzania (usually given as an example of successful language planning in Africa), the book discusses the problem of using English as a medium of education in a predominantly Kiswahili-speaking society. Drawing on the Tanzanian experience, contributors to this volume address the issue of language policy in Africa and the implications of this for the socio-economic development of the continent.

Russ, Charles, V. J. (ed.)

The dialects of modern German: a linguistic survey. Stanford, CA: Stanford University Press, 1990. xxiii+519 pp. $60.00.

A comprehensive survey of the linguistic characteristics of modern German dialects in their socio-linguistic setting, this volume is intended both for students of German who wish to deepen their knowledge of German dialects and for linguists and sociolinguists who wish to learn some of the main features of German dialects. For the latter, only an elementary knowledge of German is needed, for after each dialect form the standard German is given, followed by an English gloss.

The population upheavals during and after the Second World War greatly influenced the development and range of dialect (half a dozen dialects have vanished during this period), and in this book 11 eminent dialectologists allow the reader to follow differences in the use and form of dialect in the areas where modern German dialects are used. These areas are the Federal Republic of Germany, the German Democratic Republic, Austria, Luxemburg, German-speaking parts of Switzerland, and Alsace.

The book is in four parts, following the traditional classification of German dialects into Low, Central, and Upper German, with Frisian (actually a separate language) as a special case. For each dialect, the author examines its use and status in detail, and provides historical and geographical background, including isogloss maps. Linguistic descriptions cover the phonological system and the inflection of the noun, adjective, pronoun and verb, and illustrate word-formation, lexical features and syntax.

Phonological descriptions are in phonemic terms with full attention paid to allophonic variation; grammatical descriptions use traditional terms. Throughout the book, synchronic linguistic descriptions are used to compare the dialect forms with standard German.

Spolsky, Bernard

Conditions for second language learning: introduction to a general theory. Oxford: Oxford University Press, 1989. x+272 pp. £22.00 (£8.95 pb).

This book explores the requirements for a general theory of second language learning, and considers the relevance of such a theory for language teaching. Professor Spolsky sets out his theory in the form of a preference model, or series of typical and categorical rules or conditions. In this way he is able to account for differences both between individual language learners, and between different kinds of learning – for example, formal and informal learning, and learning for general and special purposes. The model emphasises the need to be precise and clear on the nature of the goals and outcomes of learning, and to recognise the complexity of the concept 'knowing a second language'.

Stevick, Earl W.

Humanism in language teaching. Oxford: Oxford University Press, 1990 (New Perspectives series). 162 pp. £6.95.

This study invites readers to radically reassess their understanding of the term 'humanism' in relation to language teaching. What kinds of words and word-pictures have teachers used to describe 'humanistic' approaches? What assumptions lie behind the controversies which surround these approaches? How much do we know about the thinking which lies behind the labels 'Community Language Learning' and 'Silent Way'? Are there elements of humanism in methods which are not commonly referred to as 'humanistic'?

Books received

Trudgill, Peter

The dialects of England. Oxford: Blackwell, 1990. 145 pp. £14.95.

This book celebrates the rich variety of the regional and social dialects of English in all its forms, ancient and modern. It covers Zummerzet and Scouse, Cockney and Cumberland, Brummie and Berkshire, Nottingham and Norfolk. It deplores the trend towards linguistic uniformity urged on us by the self-appointed guardians of the purity of the English language.

English dialects are the result of 1500 years of linguistic and cultural development. Written in non-technical language, this book outlines their history and their geography. It describes and delights in the diversity of vocabulary, accent, grammar and literature to be found among the dialects of England.

VanPatten, Bill and Lee, James F. (eds).

Second language acquisition – foreign language learning. Clevedon, Avon: Multilingual Matters, 1990. xii + 276 pp. £43.00 (£14.95 pb).

Through a selected integration of chapters from leading researchers in both areas, the volume explores the contexts, processes, and products that comprise the disciplines known as second language acquisition and foreign language learning. The aims of the collection are to offer various perspectives on how second language acquisition and foreign language learning come together as fields of inquiry and to suggest how foreign language teaching benefits from research in language learning.

Wajnryb, Ruth

Grammar dictation. Oxford: Oxford University Press, 1990. (Resource Books for Teachers series). 132 pp. £7.50.

This book offers an innovative approach to the study of grammar in the language classroom – the 'dictogloss' procedure. This procedure consists of the following stages: (1) listening – a text is dictated at a speed which allows only key words to be noted; (2) text reconstruction – students pool their resources to reconstruct their own version of the original text; (3) analysis – the correction process enables students to understand their errors and the language options available to them. 'Grammar dictation' and 'dictogloss' are used synonymously in this book to describe a procedure which involves teacher and students in communicative interaction, text creation or reconstruction, and error analysis.

Windisch, Uli

Speech and reasoning in everyday life. Cambridge and Paris: Cambridge University Press and Editions de la Maison des Sciences de l'Homme, 1990. x + 224 pp. £32.50.

This book examines the nature and operation of social thought and language as used in everyday life, and looks at social thinking through the complex patternings and functions of discourse. It is based on extensive empirical evidence about the language of contemporary racism and nationalism, drawn from the vast corpus of the discourse of Swiss racism gathered by the author from a variety of written and spoken sources. Three principal investigations, of sociocentrism, causality and the perception of time, are used to situate and define the nature and working of everyday speech and reasoning. Windisch analyses the patterns of discursive moves and their 'underlying logics'.

This book is a contribution to the analysis of the discourse of contemporary ideology and politics. The author criticises those psychological approaches which ignore the social dimensions of human knowledge and treat thinking purely as a matter of individual psychology. In this respect his notion of 'sociocognitive' structure resembles that of 'social representation'. However, his work is much more firmly located within the analysis of language and discourse structure than the work of most social representation theorists.

Books received

Language learning and teaching

Methods of teaching English to Arab students. N. Al-Mutawa and T. Kailani. Longman (Longman Handbooks for Teachers of English to Arab Students series), 1990. £5.95.

English pronunciation for Arabic speakers. T. F. Mitchell and S. El-Hassan. Longman (Longman Handbooks for Teachers of English to Arab Students, 1990. £5.95.

Language

Listening to spoken English (2nd edn.). G. Brown. Longman, 1990. £8.95.

Linguistics

Linguistic realities: an autonomist metatheory for the generative enterprise. P. Carr. Cambridge University Press, 1990. £25.00.

Books received

Writing

Schreit mir bitte! Letter-writing practice. D. Phillips and others. Nelson, 1990. £3.75.

Grammar

Check your English: a four-skills grammar practice book. Students' book 1, Teacher's book 1. R. MacAndrew and J. Blundell. Macmillan, 1990.

Dictionaries

Langenscheidt's standard Italian dictionary: Italian-English, English-Italian. R. C. Melzi. Langersheidt, 1990. £8.95.

Collins Spanish pocket dictionary (also *French, German, Italian*). Collins, 1990. £4.95 each.

Oxford pocket English grammar. A. J. Thomson and A. V. Martinet. Oxford University Press, 1990. £3.95.

Collins Gem dictionary and thesaurus. Collins, 1990. £2.99. Matching dictionary and thesaurus entries on the same page.

A dictionary of stylistics. K. Wales. Longman, 1990. £13.95. Over 600 entries covering sociolinguistics, semiotics, grammar, communication theory, poetics and traditional rhetoric.

Bloomsbury good word guide (2nd edn.). M. Manser (ed.). Bloomsbury, 1990. £16.99.

Longman photo dictionary activity book. J. Olerarski. Longman, 1990. £2.20.

Concordances in the classroom: a resource book for teachers. C. Tribble and G. Jones. Longman, 1990. £5.50.

Newspaper French: a vocabulary of administrative and commercial idiom. A. C. Ritchie. University of Wales Press, 1990. £15.95 (£7.95 pb).

An A to Z of British life. A. Room. Oxford University Press, 1990. £6.95. Alphabetical guide to Britain and the British way of life.

Materials

Japanese Now. Vol. 4. E. M. T. Sato and M. Sakihara. University of Hawaii Press, 1990. £22.80. Part of a 4-year sequence of curriculum materials for teaching Japanese to non-natives.

Courses

Colloquial Italian. F. Andrews. Routledge, 1990. £14.95. Book and cassette.

Formula One. H. Imbert and others. Macmillan, 1990. Workbook 1. £2.95, Teacher's book 1 £8.50, Student's book 1 £5.25. Cassette for Workbook £8.50.

English Around You. M. Potter. Macmillan, 1990. Teacher's book 1 £8.95. Resource book 1, Student's book 1. 3 cassettes, £8.50 each. A 3-level course in English as a medium of communication in a non-English speaking environment.

Experiences. S. Swift. Macmillan, 1990. Student's Book £5.25, Teacher's book. Complete course for upper intermediate level.

Insights. M. Macfarlane. Macmillan, 1990. Student's book, Workbook. Complete course for pre-FCE level.

Arc-en-Ciel stage 1: Assessment and profiling pack. T. Blee and R. Venables. Mary Glasgow Publications, 1990. Pack (repromasters, teachers' notes and cassette) £34.95. Four-stage wide ability French course.

Arc-en-Ciel stage 3. M-T. Bougard and others. Mary Glasgow Publications, 1990. Teacher's book £12.50, pupil's book £6.25, 6 cassettes £29.95 + VAT, repromasters £31.95.

New Cambridge English Course, Students Book 2. M. Swan and C. Walter. Cambridge University Press, 1990. £4.95. Part of a four-level course; this level takes students to lower intermediate level.

Literature

Beyond the 'nouveau roman': essays on the contemporary French novel. M. Tilby (ed.). Berg Publishers Ltd. £19.50.

Periodicals

Annals of the American Academy of Political and Social Sciences. March 1990: 'English plus: issues in bilingual education'. Sage Publications, £9.95.

International Journal of Sign Linguistics, **1**, 1 (1990).

Texts

Märkische Forschungen by Günter de Bruyn. Ed. by D. Tate (Manchester New German Texts). Manchester University Press, 1990. £25.00 (£6.95 pb.).

International schools

ESL: a handbook for teachers and administrators in international schools. Ed. by E. Murphy. Multilingual Matters, 1990. £25.00. Guide to setting up an ESL programme for low English proficient (LEP) children.

Bibliographies

This section presents a selective list of bibliographies taken from recent journals, and occasionally includes books or other sources.

Language learning and teaching

Didactics of Russian and other foreign languages: select bibliography for 1986. Information bulletin produced by Charles University, Prague, Central Library, Sectional Information Centre of Pedagogical Faculty, 1989 (2 parts). Annotated, 1326 entries (fifth volume in a series). Based on journal articles and reviews.

Recent Canadian publications for second language teachers. By A. Weinrib. Continuation in *Canadian Modern Language Review*, **45**, 1 (1988), 155–60.

German synonyms: a bibliography of words explaining their usage. By W. A. Benware. In *Die Unterrichtspraxis*, **22**, 1 (1989), 69–81. Covers books and articles from 1945 to 1987. 319 unannotated entries, with index of words in journal articles.

Survey of interactive language discs. By J. Rubin and others. In *CALICO Journal*, **7**, 3 (1990), 31–47 *and* 50–6. Annotated as to: language, level, language skill addressed, equipment needed, availability, etc.

Second language retention. By A. Vechter and others. Article summarising an extensive annotated bibliography. In *Canadian Modern Language Review*, **46**, 2 (1990), 289–303. [*See abstract* 90–425.]

List of abstractors

J. Baildam	School of English and Foreign Languages, Newbold College, Bracknell
R. Clift	Darwin College, Cambridge
S. Death	Formerly CILT
V. Kinsella	Editor
M. Lang	Department of Languages, Heriot-Watt University, Edinburgh
J. McCutcheon	Edinburgh
G. Owen	Portfolio English, Canterbury
H. Paddon	Central London Adult Education Institute
B. Parkinson	Institute of Applied Language Studies, University of Edinburgh
D. Pickett	London Chamber of Commerce and Industry Examinations Board
L. Sheldon	Pitman Education and Training Ltd, London

SUBJECT INDEX to Vol. 23

The numbers are those of the abstracts (the year number is omitted). Initials in brackets after the number indicate a particular language, i.e. (A) Arabic, (D) Dutch, (E) English, (F) French, (G) German, (H) Hebrew, (I) Italian, (J) Japanese, (P) Polish, (R) Russian, (S) Spanish

adults, teaching, 20, 169, 195
advanced courses, 316, 416, 476, 209 (F)
   see also tertiary education
aids
   audio-visual, 65
   aural, 202
   visual, 179, 210, 347
Arabic-speaking students, 119
Asian students, 304
assistant teachers, 47, 49, 50
Australia, 44, 229, 235, 257, 304, 326, 443
Austria, 367

background studies, 160, 198, 306, 329, 348, 470
   see also language and culture
beginners
   teaching, 326, 357
Belgium, 513
Bengali students, 323
bilingual teaching, 122, 128, 174, 178, 214, 217, 228, 275, 282, 349, 478, 489, 494, 500, 512, 514, 515
bilingualism, 41, 42, 94, 243, 245, 250, 359, 360, 364, 375, 382
blind teachers, 167

Canada, 35, 42, 91, 94, 147, 166, 178, 195, 214, 217, 309, 344, 346, 349, 391, 484, 487, 489, 491, 497
career opportunities for linguists, 117, 181, 445
Catalan language
   learning and teaching, 510
children, language development of, 95, 96, 97, 98, 99, 101, 102, 129, 237, 238, 239, 248, 249, 251, 252, 253, 368, 369, 371, 375, 378, 384, 518, 522, 524
China, 77, 170, 192
Chinese language
   learning and teaching, 509
Chinese students, 13, 70, 199, 484
commerce
   language of, 74, 106, 162, 208, 389, 485
   use of foreign languages in, 265
communication, 16, 61, 77, 171, 192, 194, 198, 219, 272, 407
   non-verbal, 326, 519, 521, 525
communicative competence, 2, 3, 4, 8, 9, 11, 104, 269, 308
community language teaching, 478
comprehension
   aural, 13, 33, 63, 90, 119, 135, 163, 244, 278, 280, 284, 288, 313, 355, 390, 464, 467, 492, 501
   reading, 68, 130, 154, 207, 236, 247, 285, 316, 421, 422, 472, 477
computer-assisted language learning, 60, 82, 88, 172, 173, 315, 320, 357, 448, 474
content-based instruction, 43, 58, 189
contrastive analysis, 116, 298, 300
   see also error analysis

conversational analysis, 103, 106, 186, 256, 362, 379, 380, 382, 527
course design, 161, 162, 199, 306, 307, 309, 407, 445, 475, 479
   evaluation, 46, 450
   see also curriculum planning, materials design, syllabus design
curriculum planning, 42, 43, 44, 160, 305, 344, 442, 443
   see also course design, materials design, syllabus design

Danish students, 459
deaf, language for the, 252
Denmark, 82
dialect, 528 (E)
dictionaries, 193 (E), 263 (F)
   see also lexicography
discourse analysis, 45, 70, 107, 194, 254, 255, 257, 338, 384, 385, 422, 422, 477, 526
   see also conversational analysis, text analysis
distance teaching, 54
drama, 171
Dutch language, 229
   learning and teaching, 440

English language, 303, 371, 386, 387, 389, 390, 421, 486
   comparative, 260, 391
   grammar, 388, 528
   in the world, 359, 516
   Received Pronunciation, 334
English language teaching, 13, 20, 32, 40, 45, 58, 63, 64, 69, 70, 71, 72, 73, 74, 75, 76, 77, 112, 118, 137, 165, 170, 176, 193, 195, 196, 197, 198, 199, 200, 201, 202, 203, 204, 205, 207, 208, 232, 274, 275, 290, 306, 309, 319, 322, 323, 326, 328, 329, 330, 331, 333, 334, 335, 336, 337, 338, 339, 340, 341, 390, 442, 454, 461, 467, 475, 476, 477, 478, 479, 480, 481, 482, 483, 484, 485, 486, 487, 488
error analysis, 101, 299, 300, 301, 433
   see also contrastive analysis
errors
   correction of, 18, 69, 168, 176, 193
Europe, 117, 181, 208, 408, 493, 513

France, 83, 114, 198, 219
French language, 53, 94, 109, 118, 301, 351, 493
   comparative, 260, 391
   grammar, 85
   learning and teaching, 35, 42, 46, 58, 78, 79, 80, 81, 82, 83, 84, 85, 86, 113, 147, 166, 171, 175, 187, 209, 210, 211, 212, 213, 214, 215, 216, 217, 264, 286, 343, 344, 345, 346, 347, 348, 349, 350, 351, 447, 468, 489, 490, 491, 492, 493, 494, 495, 496, 497
French-speaking students, 498

games, use of in language teaching, 209
German language, 102, 105, 110, 111, 118, 367, 392, 393, 394, 395
   in the world, 218
   learning and teaching, 87, 111, 117, 186, 218, 219, 220, 281, 286, 411, 498, 499
German-speaking students, 64, 488
Germany
   Federal Republic of Germany, 64, 330, 392, 512
gifted children, 142, 349
grammar
   general theory of, see under linguistics, general theory of
   teaching of, 1, 80, 111, 112, 113, 175, 184, 215, 219, 272, 310, 318, 328, 403, 458, 503 (S)
Greek language
   Classical, 225
group teaching, 88, 176

Hebrew language, 230
   learning and teaching, 131
Hindi, 359
Hong Kong, 199, 509
humour, 347

idioms, 96, 241
immigrants, 20, 83, 203, 235, 326, 413, 443, 484, 508, 512, 514
India, 336, 359
Indonesian students, 79, 309
industry
   use of foreign languages in, 117, 181, 427, 455
intensive courses, 487 (E)
interference, 298
interlanguage, 14, 16, 17, 140, 143, 277, 291, 300, 413
intermediate students, 316
international language, 197
intonation and stress, 172, 417, 386 (E), 504 (E)
Ireland, 220, 265
Irish language, 93
Israel, 190, 230, 231
Italian language
   learning and teaching, 88
Italy, 495

Japan, 207
Japanese language
   learning and teaching, 295, 352
Japanese students, 76
journalism, language of, 391

Kuwait, 201

language
   and class, 362, 381
   and culture, 64, 71, 84, 91, 118, 190, 213, 270, 306, 314, 329, 337, 346, 352, 470
   see also background studies
   and law, 255, 332

and sex, 164, 165, 363, 371, 511
and thought, 242, 253
language awareness, 514
language disorders, 140, 246
language for special purposes, 74, 115, 307, 424, 455, 467, 72 (E), 119 (E), 162 (E), 194 (E), 196 (E), 200 (E), 206 (E), 208 (E), 255 (E), 332 (E), 339 (E), 342 (E), 446 (E), 475 (E), 499 (G)
language learning and teaching, 408
methodology, *see under* methodology of language teaching
theory and principles, 1, 2, 3, 4, 5, 6, 7, 8, 9, 10, 11, 12, 18, 67, 80, 112, 113, 114, 115, 116, 117, 118, 149, 265, 266, 267, 268, 269, 270, 271, 272, 281, 297, 344, 401, 402, 403, 404, 405, 406, 407, 429, 444
see also psychology of language learning
language needs, analysis of, 265
Lebanese language
learning and teaching, 235
less able pupils, 318, 370, 376
lexicography, 263, 531
lexicology, 264
linguistic universals, 121, 127, 238, 279, 402, 412
linguistics
applications to language teaching, 1, 115, 266, 268, 297, 402, 496
description and analysis, 116, 254 (F), 394 (G), 400 (R)
general theory of, 225
neurolinguistics, 124, 226
literacy teaching, 20
literature, teaching of, 5, 75, 190, 319, 321, 322, 331, 335, 346, 476

Maori language, 233
materials design, 66, 112, 163, 164, 165, 308, 339, 446
'authentic' materials, 313, 447
evaluation, 448, 449
memory, 26, 29, 100, 145, 169, 373, 425
methodology of language teaching, 1, 7, 10, 17, 19, 43, 52, 54, 55, 56, 57, 58, 59, 60, 61, 65, 66, 67, 68, 69, 72, 85, 128, 132, 147, 169, 170, 171, 172, 174, 175, 177, 178, 180, 181, 182, 183, 184, 185, 186, 187, 189, 190, 191, 192, 193, 195, 201, 210, 219, 267, 271, 274, 275, 290, 294, 298, 311, 313, 314, 315, 317, 320, 323, 325, 326, 327, 330, 331, 336, 338, 340, 343, 346, 347, 349, 383, 403, 404, 408, 419, 455, 456, 457, 458, 459, 460, 461, 462, 463, 464, 465, 466, 469, 470, 471, 473, 474, 476, 481, 482, 483, 490, 492, 495, 502, 503, 500 (S)
see also linguistics (applications to language teaching), group teaching, distance teaching, bilingual teaching, suggestology
class methods, 64, 77, 81, 137, 168, 176, 179, 188, 316, 318, 321, 356, 163 (E), 202 (E), 339 (E), 486 (E), 53 (F), 62 (F), 78 (F), 211 (F), 350 (F), 447 (F), 468 (F), 295 (J), 89 (R),
90 (R), 221 (R), 223 (R), 224 (R), 348 (R), 354 (R), 355 (R)
see also aids, drama, drills, dictionaries, games, radio, television, textbooks, reading, writing skills, translation, video, vocabulary
minority languages, 508, 510
Morocco, 71, 125, 306
mother tongue, 125
teaching of, 212, 235, 335, 500, 83 (F)
use of for instruction, 201
mothers, language of, 522
motivation, 188, 325
multiculturalism, 470
multilingualism, 99, 125, 375, 506, 513

New Zealand, 233

oral skills, teaching
see under speech

Pakistan, 461
parents, language of, 239, 253, 524
phonetics and phonology, 18, 23, 52, 95, 172, 182, 240, 297, 505, 56 (E), 504 (E), 85 (F), 396 (R), 397 (R)
Polish language
learning and teaching, 177
Portuguese language, 227, 501
pragmatics, 102, 104, 108, 257, 258, 259, 262, 280, 379, 381, 383, 405
primary education, 213, 349
project management, 442
pronunciation, 172, 180, 182, 333, 334, 474, 209 (F)
psycholinguistics, 100, 236, 238, 240, 241, 242, 243, 244, 245, 246, 247, 248, 250, 253, 368, 369, 370, 372, 373, 374, 376, 377, 378, 385, 428, 517, 519, 520, 521, 523, 525
psychology of language learning, 12, 13, 14, 15, 16, 17, 19, 20, 22, 23, 25, 26, 27, 28, 29, 63, 119, 121, 122, 123, 124, 125, 126, 127, 128, 129, 130, 131, 132, 133, 134, 135, 136, 137, 138, 139, 140, 141, 142, 143, 145, 146, 273, 274, 275, 276, 277, 278, 279, 280, 281, 282, 283, 284, 285, 287, 288, 290, 292, 293, 294, 295, 403, 409, 410, 411, 412, 413, 414, 415, 416, 417, 418, 419, 420, 421, 422, 423, 424, 425, 430, 433, 444, 456, 457, 460, 463, 484, 488
age and L2 learning, 21, 289, 296
comparison of L1 and L2 learning, 18, 120, 144, 291
sex differences in language learning, 24, 104, 286
see also interlanguage, memory, motivation
punctuation, 260

radio, 202
reading, 27, 32, 36, 95, 150, 183, 312, 320, 322, 324, 370, 376, 423, 428, 457, 459, 461, 465, 466, 490, 517, 520
aloud, 187
see also comprehension, reading
remedial teaching
reading, 68
research methods, 18, 29, 103, 148, 149, 279, 297, 360, 426, 427, 428, 430, 462, 499
classroom-centred research, 147, 429, 431, 432
Russian language, 222, 223, 261, 262, 396, 397, 398, 399, 400
learning and teaching, 89, 90, 221, 222, 223, 224, 353, 354, 355, 356, 357
scientific and technical language, 389 (E), 393 (G)
secondary education, 35, 64, 87, 131, 181, 198, 286, 318, 319, 330, 335, 341, 358, 383, 498, 509
self-assessment, 152, 157, 435
self-directed learning, 79, 409, 469, 498
semantics, 108, 380, 387 (E), 400 (R)
sign language, 234, 252
Singapore, 516
sociolinguistics, 91, 94, 230, 232, 233, 234, 235, 257, 359, 360, 362, 363, 364, 365, 366, 367, 381, 401, 406, 426, 494, 506, 507, 508, 511, 512, 513, 516
language change, 361
language loss, 227, 229, 231
language planning, 92, 93, 218, 228, 509, 510, 514, 515
South Africa, 131, 204, 473
South America, 84
Spain, 510
Spanish language, 371, 529
learning and teaching, 358, 441, 500, 501, 502, 503
Spanish-speaking students, 16, 20, 41, 413
speech, 13, 159, 362, 474, 56 (E), 70 (E), 482 (E), 53 (F), 78 (F), 254 (F), 468 (F), 34 (G), 90 (R)
research, 240
study skills, 475
suggestology, 473
Swedish-speaking students, 421
Switzerland, 366, 494, 506, 515
syllabus design, 45, 328, 388, 444
see also course design, materials design
teacher training, 47, 48, 49, 50, 51, 166, 167, 451, 452, 453, 454
teachers
assessing performance of, 439
behaviour of, 19, 326, 429
language of, 57
style of, 12, 317
television
satellite, 355
tertiary education, 315, 424, 441
universities, 89, 162, 216, 303, 307, 343, 345, 445, 462, 497
testing, 33, 36, 37, 39, 40, 149, 150, 154, 155, 158, 302, 303, 304, 430, 437, 439, 440
communicative, 151
oral, 34, 35, 41, 153, 156, 159, 438
placement, 32, 441
proficiency, 30, 31, 35, 41, 434, 436
pronunciation, 38
text analysis, 105
textbooks, 446, 194 (E), 306 (E), 86 (F), 87 (G), 353 (R), 503 (S)

sexism in, 164, 165
training, 206, 342, 455, 485
translation, 382, 531, 532
    as a class exercise, 66, 185
    machine, 530
Turkish students, 512

Union of Soviet Socialist Republics, 341
United Kingdom, 103, 329, 358, 478, 508

United States of America, 20, 47, 49, 50, 84, 87, 92, 203, 232, 303, 424, 441, 496
    Mexican-American students, 275, 288

video, 50, 64, 89, 179, 188, 350, 468
vocabulary
    learning of, 55, 177, 183, 211, 282, 308, 433, 459, 460
    teaching of, 39, 40, 59, 137, 259, 264, 316, 340, 423, 430, 481, 502, 356 (R)

word-processor, 312
writing skills, 27, 73, 88, 123, 162, 205, 242, 251, 260, 275, 290, 292, 312, 335, 338, 383, 462, 480, 282 (F), 295 (J)
    written and spoken language compared, 374.

AUTHOR INDEX to Vol. 23

The numbers are those of the abstracts (the year number is omitted).

Adamson, H. D., 444, 475
Adaskou, K., 306
Alderson, J. Charles, 30, 150
Alexander, Louis G., 310, 328
Allen, Patrick, 42, 147
Allison, Desmond, 390
Ammon, Ulrich, 218
Andersen, Paul Kent, 225
Anderson-Hsieh, Janet, 13
Andres, Franz, 506, 515
Andrews, Barry J., 254
Antier, Maurice, 329
Appel, Joachim, 330, 331
Arnaud, Pierre J. L., 151, 434
Arndt, Horst, 455
Assbeck, Johann, 476
Atkinson, David, 311

Bachman, Lyle F., 31, 152
Bacon, Susan M., 313
Bahns, Jens, 193, 456, 488
Banerjee, Janet, 70
Bate, Michèle, 209
Batstone, Rob, 161
Beeching, Kate, 112
Beedham, Christopher, 194
Bello, Josefina, 358
Benson, Malcolm J., 119
Bensoussan, Marsha, 477
Bentahila, Abdelâli, 71, 125
Beretta, Alan, 168, 305
Berman, Ruth, 368
Berns, Margie, 401
Berry, Roger, 451
Bertoldi, Elizabeth, 195
Besse, Henri, 113
Bhatia, Tej K., 359
Bhatia, V. K., 255, 332
Bialystok, Ellen, 273, 369
Bild, Eva-Rebecca, 489
Billières, M., 52
Bim, I. L., 353
Blanche, Patrick, 435
Bloor, Meriel, 194
Bogacheva, E. M., 298
Boland, Julie E., 517
Bond, Z. S., 504
Bongaerts, Theo, 120
Bonnet, Philippe, 169
Bookbinder, David, 352
Bossé-Andrieu, Jacqueline, 109
Botha, H. Ludolph, 473
Bourne, Jill, 478
Boyd, Francis A., 47
Boyle, Joseph, 199
Brady, Susan, 370
Brenez, Michelle, 498
Brennan, Moya, 72, 196
Bresson, Daniel, 1
Brown, Adam, 333, 334
Brown, Gillian, 314
Brown, James Dean, 32
Brown, Raymond W., 452
Brunet, Jean-Paul, 78
Bryant, P. E., 95
Burnaby, Barbara, 170

Butler, Katharine, 360
Button, Graham, 103
Buxton, Barbara, 39
Byrd, Patricia, 162

Cacciari, Cristina, 96
Cahill, Desmond, 235
Caldwell, Gary, 91
Call, Mary Emily, 16
Calvé, Pierre, 48, 391
Cameron, Judy, 274
Cameron, Lynne J., 409
Canseco, Grace, 162
Caré, Jean-Marc, 171
Carlisle, Robert S., 275
Carpenter, Kathie L., 97
Carrell, Patricia L., 70, 457
Carrithers, Caroline, 236
Carroll, Susanne, 276, 410
Carton, Francis, 53, 79
Cathcart, Ruth Larimer, 45
Cazden, Courtney B., 2
Chagina, O. V., 354
Chambers, Angela, 265
Chambers, Fred, 479
Chaney, Carolyn, 237
Chapelle, Carol, 315
Charles-Luce, Jan, 518
Chartrand, Suzanne, 80
Cheng, Li-Rong, 360
Cheshire, Jenny, 379, 528
Chetouani, L., 264
Chun, Dorothy M., 172
Cicurel, Francine, 490
Cieutat-Merly, Brigitte, 219
Clahsen, Harald, 121
Clark, Eve V., 97, 368
Claverie, B., 226
Cleary, T. Anne, 441
Coates, Jennifer, 380
Cohen, Andrew D., 227, 483
Collier, Virginia P., 122
Collin, Annie, 14
Compte, Carmen, 210
Connors, Kathleen, 3
Cook, Vivian J., 15, 402
Corrales, Olga, 16
Corson, David, 160
Coste, Daniel, 312
Courtillon, Janine, 211
Cox, Brian, 335
Cox, Susan, 499
Crookall, David, 420
Crookes, Graham, 277
Cumming, Alister, 123, 148, 295, 453
Cummins, Jim, 228
Cziko, Gary A., 98

Dandonoli, Patricia, 436
Danesi, Marcel, 124
Daver, M. V., 221
David, Annie, 336
Davies, Alan, 4, 197
Davies, Catherine E., 49
Davies, Eirlys, 71, 125
Davis, James N., 54

de Kock, Josse, 458
de Bot, Kees, 229
Decotterd, Daniel, 337
de Jong, John H. A. L., 33
Delecroix, Michel, 163
Densham, Jenny, 508
Derwing, Tracey M., 278
Desmarais, C., 142
Dieckmann, Walther, 392
Dole, Robert, 73
Dollerup, Cay, 459
Douglas, Dan, 50
Dowd, Janice, 426
Dubin, Fraida, 5, 316
Dubois, Betty Lou, 530
Duda, Richard, 53, 212

Eckman, Fred R., 279
Edge, Julian, 266
Edwards, Viviane, 491
Ehlich, Susan, 280
Elkabas, Charles, 173
Elley, Warwick, 55
Ellis, Rod, 17, 281, 403, 411
Ely, Christopher M., 126
Erith, Philip, 479
Esarte-Sarries, Veronica, 213
Eubank, Lynn, 127

Faltis, Christian J., 174, 500
Felix, Sascha W., 238
Fernald, Anne, 239
Flege, James Emil, 56
Florent, Jill, 165
Fokes, Joann, 504
Fowler, Carol A., 240
Freeman, Donald, 51

Galisson, Robert, 6, 114
Gardner, R. C., 287
Gass, Susan M., 412
Gathercole, Virginia C., 371
Gayle, Grace M. H., 317
Genesee, Fred, 128
Germain, Claude, 267
Gernsbacher, Morton Ann, 372
Giacobbe, Jorge, 413
Gibbs, Raymond W., Jr., 241, 256
Gierut, Judith A., 18
Giesecke, Michael, 361
Girard, Denis, 198
Glas, C. A. W., 33
Gold, David L., 230
Gonzalez Pino, Barbara, 153
Gorbachek, A. L., 222
Görlach, Manfred, 507
Graci, Joseph P., 164
Graesser, Arthur C., 520
Green, Peter S., 269
Greene, John O., 519
Gremmo, Marie-José, 492
Grenet, Jean-Jack, 493
Gropen, Jess, 129
Grosjean, François, 427
Guberman, Solange, 60, 268
Guy, Gregory R., 92

Haastrup, Kirsten, 460
Haberlandt, Karl, 520
Hadar, Uri, 521
Hafiz, F. M., 461
Hahn, Sidney L., 34
Hajjaj, Ali H., 201
Hakansson, Gisela, 57
Hale, Gordon A., 154
Hall, Chris, 480
Hamm, Christiane, 35
Hammerly, Hector, 214
Hamp-Lyons, Liz, 302
Hansen-Strain, Lynne, 414
Harley, Birgit, 175, 282
Harlow, Linda L., 19
Harris, Roy, 242
Hartman, R. R. K., 531
Hauptman, Philip C., 58
Hayes, Elisabeth, 20
Haynes, William O., 377
Hecht, Karl-Heinz, 269
Heller, Monica, 494
Helot, Christine, 99
Hemphill, Lowry, 362
Henning, Grant, 155, 436
Herron, Carol, 294
Hicks, Deborah, 384
Higgins, John, 428
Hinz, Klaus, 318
Hirvela, Alan, 199, 319
Hodge, Bob, 257
Hoff-Ginsberg, Erika, 522
Hoffmann, Lothar, 115
Holden, Nigel J., 74, 200
Holec, Henri, 492
Holliday, Adrian, 442
Holmes, Janet, 104
Horowitz, Daniel, 462
Horsella, Maria, 292
Huckin, Thomas N., 467
Hulstijn, Jan H., 283
Hummel, Kirsten M., 260
Huspek, Michael, 381

Ibrahim, Amr Helmy, 116
Inghilleri, Moira, 338

Jackson, Linda, 343
Jacobs, George, 176
Jafarpur, Abdoljavad, 36
James, Allan R., 297
Jenkins, Joseph R., 59
Jensen, John B., 501
John, David G., 445
Johnson, Janice, 243
Johnson, Jo Ellen, 87
Johnson, Neal F., 100
Jones, Gary M., 446
Jones, Sabine, 270
Jonz, Jon, 284, 437
Jordan, R. R., 339
Jung, Matthias, 393
Jungblut, Gertrud, 463

Kasatkin, L. L., 396
Kassai, Georges, 363
Kelly, Michael H., 386
Kelly, Peter, 177
Kenkel, James M., 303
Kennedy, Barbara L., 21
Kerim-Zade, Irina, 340

Kharma, Nayef N., 201
Kilborn, Kerry, 244
King, Charlotte P., 447
King, Mary Lou, 282
Klaus, Hilde, 110
Kline, Rebecca R., 81
Knyazyev, Yu. P., 398
Koda, Keiko, 130, 285
Koehler, Kenneth, 13
Kohlmann, Ute, 105
Köpcke, Klaus-Michael, 394
Kornum, Lis, 82
Koshanova, N. I., 90
Kostromina, M. V., 223
Kraemer, Roberta, 131
Krashen, Stephen, 415
Kuznyetsova, N. G., 397

Ladefoged, Peter, 505
Lamy, André, 215
Laufer, Batia, 433, 481
Leaver, Betty Lou, 43, 355
LeBlanc, Raymond, 60, 344
Lee, Barbara, 156
Legenhausen, Lienhard, 448
Lehmann, Denis, 320
Lemmon, Christian R., 245
Lennon, Paul, 416
Leonard, Laurence B., 246
Le Page, R. B., 365
Lepetit, Daniel, 417
Leroux, Janice A., 349
Levorato, Maria Chiara, 96
Lewis, C., 178
Liebelt, Wolf, 179
Lightbown, Patsy M., 487
Lindberg, Inger, 57
Lindholm, John, 180
Linnville, Steven E., 40
Little, Greta D., 61
Lodares Marrodan, Juan Ramón, 502
Lodge, Anthony, 216
Longacre, Robert E., 526
Lötscher, Andreas, 106
Loulidi, Rafik, 286
Luce, Paul A., 518
Lukmani, Yasmeen, 150
Lund, Randall J., 464
Lynch, Brian K., 37, 449

Macaruso, Paul, 247
MacIntyre, P. D., 287
MacKinnon, Kenneth, 508
MacLaren, Richard I., 248
Magnan, Sally Sieloff, 345
Major, Roy C., 38
Man-Siu Yau, 509
March, Cynthia, 89
Marchand, Frank, 83
Markham, Paul L., 87
Mar-Molinero, Clare, 510
Marsh, Stella, 181
Martin, Jean-Pol, 62
Matthews, Margaret, 438
May, John D., 258
McCrory, D. P., 321
McDonough, Jo, 429
McDonough, Steven, 429
McKee, David, 234
McKoon, Gail, 373
McLean, Alice Musick, 468

Meara, Paul, 39, 430
Meier, Gerhard E. H., 387
Merino, Barbara J., 435
Miles, Cecil, 529
Misuono, Suesue, 315
Mitchell, Claudia A., 346
Mitchell, Keith, 388
Mitchell, Rosamond, 431
Moeller, Paulette, 166
Moirand, Sophie, 490
Mollica, Anthony, 124
Monk, Bruce, 341
Morgan, James L., 22, 249
Morrison, Bruce, 202
Morrow, Philip R., 389
Motteram, Gary J., 465
Mulac, Anthony, 511
Müller, Frank, 382
Murphey, Tim, 418
Murphy, John M., 63
Murtagh, Lelia, 466
Muysken, Pieter, 121
Myers, Cindy, 50
Myers, Marie J., 132
Myers-Scotton, Carol, 364

Nagy, William, 378
Nation, Paul, 482
Nehr, Monika, 512
Nelde, Peter Hans, 513
Neufeld, Gerald G., 23
Neville, Grace, 347
Niccols, Alison, 369
Nice, Richard, 343
Nickel, Gerhard, 299
Nobili, Paola, 495
Nunan, David, 44, 443
Nünning, Ansgar, 322
Nyikos, Martha, 134

Ó Ciosáin, Séamus, 93
Oksaar, Els, 250
Olsen, Leslie A., 467
Olsen, Roger E. W-B., 203
Olshtain, Elite, 231, 483
O'Malley, J. Michael, 288
Orban, Clara, 468
Oscarson, Mats, 157
Oster, Judith, 75
Osterhout, Lee, 523
Oxford, Rebecca L., 24, 133, 134, 419, 420

Palmberg, Rolf, 421
Palmer, Adrian S., 152
Panther, Klaus-Uwe, 394
Pap, Leo, 366
Paper, Li Chuang, 484
Paret, Marie-Christine, 80
Parke, Tim, 323
Patkowski, Mark S., 289
Pavlov, Vladimir, 340
Pearson, Lon, 474
Peirce, Bronwyn Norton, 204
Pelfrène, Arnaud, 320
Pennington, Martha C., 182, 439
Pennycook, Alastair, 404
Perkins, Kyle, 40
Pestre de Almeida, Lilian, 84
Pica, Teresa, 25
Pienemann, Manfred, 135

Pitts, Michael, 183
Polomska, Margaret, 136
Porcher, Louis, 324
Porte, Graeme, 137
Poulisse, Nanda, 120, 138
Prabhu, N. S., 271
Puhl, C. A., 307
Puren, Christian, 469
Py, Bernard, 405

Querbach, Carl W., 85
Quetz, Jurgen, 184

Ragan, Peter H., 205
Rahilina, E. V., 399
Ralph, Edwin G., 325
Rampton, Ben, 514
Rampton, M. B. H., 406
Raphael, Taffy E., 290
Reeves, Nigel, 117
Rehorick, Sally, 491
Ressler, Michael, 111
Rey, Alain, 263
Ricciardelli, Lina A., 139
Richards, Keith, 7, 206, 342
Richardson, Ian M., 185, 422
Rings, Lana, 186
Rivenc-Chiclet, M.-M., 86
Robb, Thomas N., 207
Robert, Jean Michel, 140
Robin, Richard M., 355
Robinson, Peter J., 259, 308
Romney, J. C., 187
Rose, Sheila D., 470
Royster, Linda, 485
Rubenfield, Stephen A., 424
Rubin, Donald L., 374
Rubin, Hyla, 251
Rusch, Paul, 367
Rutherford, William E., 291
Ryabova, A. E., 224

Sagarra, Eda, 220
Saleemi, Anjum P., 141
Sanders, Sara L., 61
Sandra, Dominiek, 26
Sankaran Unni, K. P., 261
Sarig, Gissi, 158
Sato, Charlene J., 232
Savage, Fiona J., 326
Savignon, Sandra J., 407
Schils, Erik, 138
Schinke-Llano, Linda, 375
Schleppegrell, Mary, 485
Schmidt, Herminio, 188
Schneider, Judith Morganroth, 348
Schneiderman, E. I., 142

Schoorl, J. J., 440
Schouten-van Parreren, Caroline, 423
Sciarone, A. G., 440
Seidler, Klaus W., 64
Selinker, Larry, 300
Shaffer, Constance, 471
Shapson, Stan M., 178
Sharp, Alastair, 450
Shibles, Warren, 395
Side, Richard, 486
Sinderman, Gerda, 292
Sinyor, Roberta, 88
Sivenko, M. O., 356
Slimani, Assia, 432
Smith, D., 309
Smith, Maureen M., 349
Smith, Suzanne T., 376
Snow, Marguerite Ann, 189
Snyder, Helena Romano, 65
Spada, Nina, 487
Spenney, Maria J., 377
Spolsky, Bernard, 8, 233
Spolsky, Ellen, 190
Stalker, James C., 9
Stemberger, Joseph Paul, 101
Stephens, Doris T., 350
Stone, Gregory B., 424
Stotz, Daniel, 515
Stryker, Stephen B., 43
Surridge, Marie, 351
Susser, Bernard, 207
Swaffar, Janet K., 149
Swain, Merrill, 148, 489
Swartz, J. J., 307
Swinney, David A., 523
Swisher, M. Virginia, 234, 252

Taft, Ronald, 235
Takashima, Hideyuki, 76
Tauroza, Steve, 390
Tay, Mary W. J., 516
Tenjoh-Okwen, Thomas, 143
Terrell, Tracy David, 503
Terry, Robert, 301
Thomas, Margaret, 144, 293
Tierney, Robert J., 27
Tomasello, Michael, 294, 524
Tosi, Arturo, 208
Trafford, John, 167
Travis, Lisa L., 249
Trim, John, 408
Trimboli, Antonietta, 525
Tucker, Richard W., 303
Tudor, Ian, 66, 461, 472
Tuman, Walter Vladimir, 357
Tyler, Andrea, 378

Ulichny, Polly, 383
Ullman, Roberta, 46
Underhill, Adrian, 327
Uspensky, M. B., 298
Üzawa, Kozue, 295

Valdés, Guadalupe, 41
Valdman, Albert, 496
van der Vyver, Dawid H., 473
van Els, Theo, 29
van Essen, Arthur, 272
van Lier, Leo, 159
van Naerssen, Margaret, 72, 196
VanPatten, Bill, 28
Vechter, Andrea, 425
Vigner, Gérard, 191
Vila, Joaquin, 474
Vogel, Thomas, 488
Vsyevolodova, M. V., 262

Waddell, Eric, 94
Wagner, Johannes, 67
Walker, Ann Arnaud, 68
Walker, Michael B., 525
Wallace, Ruth, 428
Walter, Catherine, 165
Watson, Rita, 253
Watson-Gegeo, Karen Ann, 383
Watts, Richard J., 107
Weber, Ursula, 102
Weinrich, Harald, 118
Weltens, Bert, 29, 145
Wesche, M. B., 497
Westphal, Germán, 296
Wherritt, Irene, 441
White, Cynthia J., 77, 192
Widdowson, H. G., 10, 11
Wildner-Bassett, Mary E., 527
Wilensky, Robert, 108
Williams, K. L., 304
Wilss, Wolfram, 532
Wiss, Corrinne, 217
Wolf, Dennie, 384
Wolff, Dieter, 448
Woods, Devon, 69
Woodward, Tessa, 454
Wright, Peter, 385

Yilin Sun, 170
Young, Aileen L., 439

Zisenwine, David, 131
Zobl, Helmut, 146
Zolotova, G. A., 400
Zuber-Skerritt, Ortrun, 12

JOURNAL OF MULTILINGUAL and MULTICULTURAL DEVELOPMENT

Editor: Derrick Sharp *Review Editor:* Colin Williams

Editorial Board:
Adebisi Afolayan, H. Baetens Beardsmore, W. Butzkamm, Michael Byram, Maurice Craft, Jim Cummins, Carl J. Dodson, Carol M. Eastman, John Edwards, Howard Giles, François Grosjean, Jagdish S. Gundara, Godfrey Harrison, Gottfried Kolde, Mildred L. Larson, Christer Laurén, P. H. Nelde, John Platt, Miguel Siguan, T. Skutnabb-Kangas, Alan Thomas.

This journal, with its truly international editorial board, has done much to further the course of multilingual and multicultural studies in the ten years since it was first published. It has ranged widely in its interests and is now especially keen to extend its range by publishing more articles and research studies in the areas of cultural and intercultural studies. It will of course continue to publish papers on all aspects of bilingualism and multilingualism, and of the rights and obligations of minorities, from many different points of view.

Over the years we have been very pleased to hear the comment along the lines: "This is the one journal where I read all the papers".

Details of recent issues:

Vol. 10 No. 1, 1989. Special Issue on Bilingualism and Bilingual Education in Friesland
Guest Editor: Koen Zondag
- Diversity and Uniformity in Six Bilingual Schools in Friesland; *K. Zondag*
- Language and Literacy Acquisition in Bilingual Contexts; *J. Cummins*
- Psycholinguistic Aspects of Bilingualism; *E. Oksaar*
- The Identity of a Minority; *K. Liebkind*
- Ethnic Minority Languages Versus Frisian in Dutch Primary Schools: A Comparative Perspective; *G. Extra*
- Ecological Aspects of Language Contact or How to Investigate Linguistic Minorities; *P. H. Nelde*

Vol. 10 No. 4, 1989
- Jewish–Canadian Ethnic Identity and Non-native Language Learning: A Social Psychological Study; *G. Feuerverger*
- Language as a Social Problem: The Repression of Spanish in S. Texas; *A. Hurtado & R. Rodriguez*
- Language Education in Changing Economic and Political Context: The Teaching of Putonghua in Hong Kong Schools; *Ora W. Y. Kwo*
- The Controversy over Teaching Medium in Hong Kong: Analysis of a Language Policy; *Y. Man Siu*
- Migrant Literature in Intercultural Education; *S. Luchtenberg*
- The Teaching of Catalan in Catalonia; *C. Mar-Molinero*
- Work in Progress; Book Reviews

Vol. 11 Nos 1 & 2, 1990
Special Issue on Fourth International Conference on Minority Languages
Guest Editors: Durk Gorter et al.

Volume 11 (1990) 6 issues Libraries/Institutions £63.00 (US$130.00)
Individuals £21.00 (US$45.00) Students £11.00 (US$24.00)

Payment may be made by
ACCESS/MASTERCARD/EUROCARD/AMERICAN EXPRESS/DINER'S CARD

 **MULTILINGUAL MATTERS LTD**
Bank House, 8a Hill Road, Clevedon
Avon, England, BS21 7HH

University of Cambridge

Summer Institute in English and Applied Linguistics

Language and Understanding

A two-week residential course for university or college lecturers, teacher trainers and senior teachers of English

14 – 27 July 1991

Director: Gillian Brown

The speakers will include:

Jean Aitchison　　　Ellen Bialystok
Keith Brown　　　　Lesley Milroy
Bernard Spolsky　　Deirdre Wilson

For details: Richard Mason, Madingley Hall, Madingley,
Cambridge CB3 8AQ, England. Tel: (UK) 954 210636; Fax: (UK) 954 210677

A Way with Words 2
Vocabulary development activities for learners of English
Stuart Redman and **Robert Ellis**
Advisory Editor: **Michael McCarthy**

NEW

Your students ask:

'How can I learn more vocabulary?'

A Way with Words provides the answers through a learner-centred and creative approach to vocabulary learning.

A Way with Words 2 is now available.

Contents include:

- Connecting words and ideas
- Looking after yourself
- Ways of looking at things

With *A Way with Words* vocabulary learning is fun!

For further information on Cambridge ELT publications, please contact ELT Marketing, Cambridge University Press, The Edinburgh Building, Shaftesbury Road, Cambridge CB2 2RU, UK.
Tel: (0223) 325846/7.

CAMBRIDGE UNIVERSITY PRESS